MARX ON GLOBALISATION

MARX ON GLOBALISATION

Edited and Selected by

DAVID RENTON

Lawrence & Wishart
LONDON

Lawrence and Wishart Limited
99a Wallis Road
London
E9 5LN

First published 2001

British Library Cataloguing in Publication Data.
A catalogue record for this book is available from the
British Library

ISBN 0 85315 909-2

Typeset in Liverpool by Derek Doyle & Associates
Printed and bound by The Bath Press, Bath

Website address www.l-w-bks.co.uk

CONTENTS

SECTION 6: COMMODITIES AND CONSUMERISM

SECTION 7: CAPITAL, MONEY, WAGES AND TRADE

SECTION 8: CAPITAL, FINANCE AND PROFIT

SECTION 9: LABOUR

If not otherwise indicated the footnotes are by Marx or Engels. Editorial footnotes are taken from the sources listed at the beginning of each section.

INTRODUCTION
MARX ON GLOBALISATION

Globalisation, as a process, has a long history, the creation and expansion of the United Nations and many other multinational organisations, steady growth in world commerce, development of internationalised knowledge systems in symbiosis with social evolution – implying changed patterns of communication, technology, production and consumption, and the promotion of internationalism as a cultural value. Few sections of the global population escaped the effects of two world wars and the Depression between them, despite wide differences in the various degrees of participation or even interest. The technological revolution lies at the heart of an accelerating globalisation process; it has introduced fundamental changes in the international system. International market forces increasingly shape economies and national cultures. Capital, information, and images flow around the globe at the speed of light. Trade, finance, science and technology, mass media, consumer patterns, and social and environmental problems are all globalising swiftly.

Independent Commission on Population and the
Quality of Life, 1996[1]

What is globalisation? For writers situated across the political spectrum, globalisation theory offers the most convincing account of the economic changes which shape the world today. In Britain, the *Financial Times* perceives a world market liberated from 'constraints of time, place and currency'. In the *Guardian*, Larry Elliott argues that 'the globalised market and new technologies have put an end to the idea of a job for life.' For Naomi Klein, George Monbiot and the anticapitalists of the global protest movement, the term globalisation conjures up images of a nightmarish society, manipulated by a tiny number of mega-corporations, including Coke, Pepsi, MacDonalds and Nike.[2] Indeed, what began as an economic argument has not stopped there. Globalisation is now the concept of the hour in the social sciences as well. According to one sociologist, globalisation is *the* phrase of the 1990s, 'a key idea by which we understand the transition of human society into the third millennium'. Martin Walker, the historian of the Cold War, predicts a new stage in human history, distinguished from previous epochs by 'the extraordinary global economy which will dominate our future'.[3] According to Walker, globalisation will transform our art, our culture, our literature, indeed our very conceptions of ourselves. If he is correct, then globalisation will decide the character of the world in the millennium to come.

Yet among the proponents of globalisation, there is no clear uniformity of view. Some describe globalisation as a completed event, others as a process which has hardly begun. There was no first globaliser to limit the terms of subsequent debate. Different writers emphasise different themes according to their own position in society and their opinion of what globalisation should be like. Much of the debate on globalisation takes place within global institutions, including the World Bank and the International Monetary Fund, the United Nations and the International Labour Organisation. Naturally institutions which already have a world role are sensitive to questions of global development. Meanwhile, academic sociologists have their own vision of globalisation in which their greatest hope is that work is coming to an end. Private companies tend to understand the globalisation process as one which is creating an international global marketplace, dominated by their products, Microsoft, Coke, McDonald's and Ford.

CONTEMPORARY THEORIES OF GLOBALISATION

Cultural, economic and political variants

There are at least three distinctions which can usefully be made between different approaches to the globalisation debate. The first is a contrast of subject between cultural, economic and political theories of globalisation. Clearly these approaches are linked, but different writers focus on different aspects of the argument.

Many of the cultural globalisers restrict themselves to the observation that the world is becoming more homogeneous. Cheap travel and new methods of communications are reducing the importance of national distinctions. According to Masao Miyoshi, 'National culture is increasingly irrelevant; multi-culturalism holds the day'.[4] Societies and cultures, politics and economics are coming closer together. This is Anthony Giddens' definition of globalisation: 'the intensification of worldwide social relations which link distant localities in such a way that local happenings are shaped by events occurring many miles away and vice versa'.[5] These cultural conceptions of globalisation can be characterised as being both loose and broad. Ulf Hannerz describes the world as a network of social relationships, 'and between its different regions there is a flow of meanings as well as people and goods'.[6] In John Tomlinson's phrase, 'the effects of globalisation are to weaken the cultural coherence of all individual nation states'.[7] People, goods, information and images flow between different nations at will. The world of production is becoming globalised, work becoming less important, and consumption more important. The old producer societies are dead, argues Zygmunt Bauman: 'The way present day society shapes its members is dictated first and foremost by the need to play the role of the consumer'.[8] James Martin identifies globalisation as one of a family of linked trends, including the decline of class politics, the rise of new social movements, a growing disenchantment with reason and the decline of the nation state. Thus globalisation is one of several processes leading towards a new, postmodern world.[9]

In contrast to the theorists of cultural change, those who describe political globalisation look to the sphere of international relations. Here the argument is that the emergence of global institutions has reduced the space for initiative on behalf of the nation state. Jürgen Habermas, the Frankfurt School philosopher, claims that any state 'can no longer count on its own forces to provide its citizens with adequate protection from the external effects of decisions taken by *other* actors, or from the knock-on effects of processes originating beyond its borders'.[10] The result is a democratic deficit, expressed in the rebirth of aggressive populist movements. A similar point is made by John Gray:

'A worldwide free market is no more self-regulating than the national free markets of the past'. Gray predicts the emergence of regional and international bodies of regulation – the alternative, he fears, is a return to the political upheavals of the 1930s.[11] Writing from a different perspective, rooted in the experience of the third world, Susan Strange bemoans 'the new world of debt', in which the majority of states find their policies decided by international bodies, the regional development banks, the World Bank and the IMF.[12]

Perhaps it is the theorists of economic globalisation who offer the most coherent picture of the new world which has begun to emerge since the end of the Cold War. For example, Nigel Harris's *The End of the Third World* welcomes the new global market, claiming that it will finally erode the distinction between first and third world countries. The poverty of the third world will enable its producers to compete. Thanks to the invisible hand of the free market, industry has already begun to relocate to those areas where labour is cheap. New methods of flexible working rely less on fixed means of production, and are consequently easier to move. Beyond global production according to Harris, there stands the hopeful prospect of inter-regional economic equality.[13] Other writers emphasise the new so-called 'weightless' techniques of flexible manufacture, which enable the movement of industrial production. Finance is becoming more important than industry, argue Scott Lasch and John Urry in their description of today's 'disorganised capitalism'. States, tariffs, trade unions are each alike unable to prevent capital from moving wherever it wants. In the era of globalisation, everything is changed. A truly global economy has emerged, in which huge multinational companies relocate their investment at will.[14]

Optimists and pessimists

A second division within globalisation theory lies between those who welcome the new changes, and those who are more hostile to them. While Nigel Harris is clearly optimistic, many of the other theorists are pessimistic. They accept globalisation as a fact, but describe it as a process with mostly negative consequences. Such pessimistic authors emphasise the pressure on ordinary people, who find it difficult to resist the tendency of capital to migrate towards the lowest wages and the worst conditions. Factories are being closed where labour is expensive and reopened where it is cheap. Compete or die, workers are told, global capital has won. For these writers, globalisation means disempowerment, the defeat of radical or popular forces. One such author, Robert Ross, contrasts the 'New Leviathan' of globalised capital to the 'Old Leviathan' of the state bureaucracy:

> The characteristic terror of the Old Leviathan was the police power of the state. The characteristic terror of the New Leviathan is unemployment, wage cuts, the fear that a family or a community's aspirations for environmental or economic improvement may cause the agents of the New Leviathan to take their investments to some other place where working people are more vulnerable to the demands of their employers.[15]

In a similar fashion, Kim Moody's *Workers in a Lean World* identifies the spread of globalised production with the change in work from mass to flexible production. Although sceptical of 'globaloney', Moody comes down on the side of pessimism. The distressing side of his account is not so much the rise of global production (which he disputes), but the continued crisis of capital accumulation and the consequent spread of new patterns of flexible production: 'the recipe for decentralising production processes through the creation of extended production chains of progressively lower-paying work sites and casualised labor is contributing to a deepening social crisis of the working class that began over two decades ago and shows no sign of relenting'. Thus in Moody's account, the results of globalisation are down-sizing, out-sourcing and flexible working, managerial euphemisms for an ongoing assault on behalf of capital.[16]

Sceptics and believers
A third distinction exists between those who accept globalisation as

a reality, and those who deny that a new economic order has emerged. As well as the authors listed above, most of whom accept that globalisation has taken place, there are sceptics, who do not agree that globalisation represents a new economic order. In this way, Paul Hirst and Grahame Thompson suggest that the economy is no more globalised today than it was one hundred years ago. Despite the myths, genuine trans-national corporations remain rare. There is no trend towards a greater amount of foreign investment. The world economy is not global but regional, and is dominated by just three large blocs, Europe, Japan and North America. Hirst and Thompson do not suggest that there have been no changes in the world economy. They accept that financial markets are less subject to regulation, and they also agree that there is evidence of more regional trade in manufactured and semi-manufactured goods. Yet these modest processes of change are nothing like the new economic order which the strict globalisers depict. There has always been international trade, Hirst and Thompson insist, and there is no evidence at all of a new trend towards international production. Consequently the last thirty years have seen no transfer of power up or down, no significant change.[17] Although some form of glob-alisation has undoubtedly taken place, how this process develops and how its effects are experienced, are still up for grabs. No process of change is inevitable, and every social force is open to resistance.

The sceptics are especially critical of those interpretations of global-isation that see no alternative to capitalism. Insisting that there is no other way beyond the market, implies that we should give up the search for other forms of social organisation. In this sense, they argue, the globalisation thesis can be politically disabling.

MARX ON WORLD CAPITALISM

This book is a collection of articles written by Karl Marx and Frederick Engels, including private letters, journalism, unpublished drafts of later publications, manifestos and extracts from their economic work. Although the title of the book refers to Marx, and most of the extracts are taken from his published books, Engels' writing is also included. The two were collaborators; many of their books were published together and several of Marx's later works were published under Engels' editorship after Marx's death. The intention is that readers will be able to see for themselves the approach which Marx and Engels might have brought to debates on globalisation. I have not been able to find any occasion on which either used the word globalisation, precisely because the term is a recent invention. Yet, despite the argument of many globalisation theorists that the world has now entered into a new economic era, most commentators would agree that many of the processes being analysed today go back to the old international economy, which has been with us for some time. Such processes as world capitalism, market trade between regions, the growth of finance and new patterns of work, have been part of our life since at least the 1840s, when Marx and Engels began to write.

There are several reasons therefore to return to the work of Karl Marx. One is that Marx wrote in a clear and vivid language. Most of the time, he was writing for workers and other economic lay people. His books and pamphlets are remarkably free of that jargon which disfigures much academic work. What is more, Marx and Engels were among the first writers to recognise the novelty of global capitalism, and to write about it in a systematic way. They were the first to understand that this way of doing things would expand, and that the capitalist society would spread – in their day it only existed in parts of England and Northern Europe. Given the rural and monarchical societies which they knew, whose populations lived on the land in conditions still shaped by feudalism, it was an extraordinary achievement to map out the contours of the capitalist world in which we have since come to live. As Eric Hobsbawm writes, 'Marx and Engels did not describe the world as it had already been transformed by capitalism in 1848; they predicted how it was logically destined to be transformed by it'.[18]

Marx and Engels were among the first writers to treat the international economy as a dynamic category, in which both states and regions were affected by international trends. In this way, they were close to the themes of today's globalisers who have a vision of a unified world capitalism, in which each part of the system replicates the whole. The first section of this book, 'The World Economy', includes a well-known excerpt from the *Communist Manifesto* (1848), in which the young Marx and Engels recognised the radicalism of the new capitalist order,

> All fixed, fast-frozen relations, with their train of ancient and venerable prejudices and opinions, are swept away, all new-formed ones become antiquated before they ossify. All that is solid melts into air, all that is holy is profaned, and man is at last compelled to face with sober senses his real conditions of life and his relations with his kind ... The need of a constantly expanding market for its products chases the bourgeoisie over the whole surface of the globe. It must nestle everywhere, settle everywhere, establish connections everywhere.

This passage is famous for the positive tone in which these revolutionaries celebrated the vigour of the capitalist system. Indeed it is one of the small ironies of the 1990s, that when the World Bank was looking to justify the introduction of the market into the countries of the former Communist bloc, the bank chose this passage to introduce its 1996 *World Development Report*.[19]

One form of the globalisation argument is that recent developments constitute *progress*. If anyone protests then they are simply standing in the way of scientific advance, like the King Canute of British legend who attempted and failed to turn back the waves. From this insight, it follows that is both reactionary and pointless to complain. The invisible hand of the market will necessarily allocate resources fairly across the globe. In their own day, Marx and Engels were contemptuous of those free traders and others who portrayed capitalism as operating in such a simply-positive way. Writing in 1844, Engels was scathing of those who claimed that what would come was necessarily for the best. 'You have destroyed the small monopolies so that the *one* great monopoly, property, may function the more freely and unrestrictedly,' he wrote. 'You have civilised the ends of the earth to win new terrain for the development of your vile avarice. You have brought about the fraternisation of the peoples – but your fraternity is the fraternity of thieves'.[20] The second section of this book, 'Progress', includes a passage from Marx's *Capital, Volume 1* (1867), which describes the origins of the industrial capitalist. There is also an 1848 speech from Marx in which the young radical makes clear his contempt towards both backward-looking protectionism and supposedly-progressive free trade.

It is a criticism often levelled at Marxism that Marx and Engels believed that the entire world would follow one pattern of development. According to such critics as Karl Popper, Marx believed in the inevitability of first capitalism and then socialism, and this means that Marxism is a closed historical theory, a teleology which cannot be disproved by events in the outside world.[21] Although Marx's work was more subtle and less deterministic than this, Popper's criticisms could easily be applied – and much more sharply – to globalisation theory. The claim that globalisation is inevitable is much more often asserted than it is proved.

The third section, 'The Inevitability of Development?', asks whether Marx and Engels did actually believe in the inevitability of one pattern of economic change. The argument here is that they did not. In the preface to Volume 1 of *Capital*, Marx argued that every European country was likely to undergo the same process of capitalist development, which until then had only taken place in Britain: 'It is not a question of the higher or lower degree of development of the social antagonisms that result from the natural laws of capitalist production. It is a question of these laws themselves, of these tendencies working with iron necessity towards inevitable results. The country that is more developed industrially only shows, to the less developed, the image of its own future'.[22] Later, however, Marx was more wary of using such a language of necessary change. In a famous letter to Vera Zasulich (1881), Marx suggested that Russia could by-pass capitalism. The peasantry had not been driven from the countryside, and until they were, there was no need for Russia to follow the west European model based on a land-less proletariat. This book includes a draft of the Zasulich letter, as well as an earlier letter to the Russian paper, *Otechestvenniye*

Zapiski (1877): 'By studying each of these evolutions on its own, and then comparing them, one will easily discover the key to the phenomenon, but it will never be arrived at by employing the all-purpose formula of a general historico-philosophical theory whose supreme virtue consists in being supra-historical'.[23]

Perry Anderson, among others, has criticised the Zasulich letter for its implied vision 'of a direct transition from the Russian village commune to socialism'. What Marx's account here lacks is an explanation of *how* society might advance from a primitive economic egalitarianism to an advanced industrial socialism. You might say that there is a tension within Karl Marx's theory of economic development. On the one hand, Marx believed that the world was moving in one direction, towards a more integrated global capitalism. On the other hand, he was also alive to the unevenness of this process, and to the possibility of contrary outcomes. After Marx's death, several writers would attempt to combine these insights in the theory of 'combined and uneven development'. According to this argument, capitalism was spreading even to the underdeveloped countries. Indeed the system which developed in such countries was often capitalism at its most advanced. Whole stages of historical development, which took hundreds of years in Germany or Britain, could be skipped in America, Russia and elsewhere.[24] A similar process can be seen in the recent spread of computer technology to Africa. In such countries as Egypt or South Africa, there are few schools with computers, and essential skills, including network management and computer maintenance, remain rare. Yet the latest computer languages are available, animation, web-page design and other technologies are as advanced as anything to be found in the West. This debate is one which could usefully be revisited.

It is not only Marx's account of the radical nature of capitalism which is of relevance to the debates about globalisation. Within Marx and Engels' work, there is also a sustained account of the relationship between different regions under capitalism. Although several globalisation theorists, including Nigel Harris, have argued that world capitalism will bring the third world up to the same level of development as the richest western countries, Marx was less optimistic that change would take place in this way. Section four, on 'Imperialism', includes examples of Marx's journalism from the 1850s on this theme. Two points stand out.

First, Marx argued that there was a connection between developments in the East and class struggle in the colonial countries. Both were aspects of a total system of social relationships, and there was no necessary reason why the behaviour of the West should lead the East, rather than vice versa. Writing of China in 1853, Marx maintained that 'the next uprising of the peoples of Europe ... may depend more probably on what is now passing in the Celestial Empire than on any other cause that now exists'.[25]

Second, although Edward Said has portrayed Karl Marx as a 'Romantic Orientalist' who encouraged British colonialism, Marx was alive to the brutality of the Empire. He sympathised with the misery of ordinary Indians and openly sided with them during the Indian wars of independence of 1857-9, which was a rare position in Britain at the time! Marx's 1857 article for the *New York Daily Tribune*, 'The Future Results of British Rule in India', is included here. Marx did argue that imperialism would bring to the non-industrial countries the advantages of capitalist technology, railways and new methods of production. Yet rather than taking these developments as an example of progress, he portrayed these positive developments as part of the same process as the tortures and humiliation of colonial rule. Indeed, he compared them to 'that hideous pagan idol who would not drink the nectar but from the skulls of the slain'.[26]

One of the themes of globalisation is that scientific development must necessarily introduce social change. Thus the introduction of new technology, including new media, computers and the internet, must inevitably change the way in which people live and work. Although Marx and Engels are often described as economic determinists, who would presumably accept the logic of such an argument, both were in fact sceptical of this approach. As Marx pointed out in his philosophical writings, such crude materialism deprives people of their role as agents with a power over their own future. His belief was that economic changes shaped social life, but they did not determine its condition. Section five includes the whole of Marx's 'Theses on Feuerbach' (1845): 'The materialist doctrine concerning the changing of circumstances and upbringing forgets that circumstances are changed by men and that the educator must himself be educated'. Human beings may not act under conditions of their own choosing, but they do make their own history. According to Marx, there was an interaction between base and superstructure, with the economic base shaping society, and society then re-shaping its economic base.[27]

Another of the arguments associated with globalisation is the claim that with the decline of work there will be a new society, in which everything becomes a commodity and human beings are defined by what we consume, rather than what we produce. The sixth section, 'Commodities and consumerism', contains several passages from Marx in which he argues that it is impossible to find freedom in the realm of consumption. Marx's argument was that workers were alienated at work, 'The more the worker by his labour *appropriates* the external world, sensuous nature, the more he deprives himself of *means of life*'. The alienation which began in the sphere of work then spread like a poison until it had infected every aspect of life. Money, the supposed agent of freedom in consumption, became under capitalism a source of unfreedom, a chain. As Marx argued in his 1844 *Economic and Philosophical Manuscripts*, 'The distorting and confounding of all human and natural qualities, the fraternisation of impossibilities – the *divine* power of money – lies in its *character* as men's estranged, alienating and self-disposing *species-nature*. Money is the alienated *ability of mankind*'. This section also includes a less well-known article on 'Bread Manufacture', published in the German newspaper *Die Presse* in 1862. Here Marx argued that despite scientific advances, new technology was not always introduced when it should have been. As long as it was cheaper to produce poisonous, adulterated bread, the old methods would be retained. He describes capitalist profit as a permanent obstacle standing in the way of human development, ensuring that the liberating promises of modern technology were not met: 'Wherever we look, we shall find that the most immediate needs have thus far avoided the influence of large-scale industry, with more or less obstinacy, and their satisfaction depends upon the hopelessly detailed craft methods of ancient tradition'.[28]

The seventh section, 'Capital, money, wages and trade', is made up of extracts from Marx's *Capital* and from Marx's economic manuscripts. Several of these directly contradict the economic claims which lie behind globalisation theory. One of the globalisers' claims is that labour price is a determining factor which decides the price of a commodity. From this it follows that production should move to the country where labour is cheapest. In *Capital 1*, Marx demonstrated that this argument is a fiction. The price of labour is only one of the factors which decide the cost of a product, and manufacture is not necessarily cheaper where labour finds its lowest reward. Indeed, where there is the most advanced machinery, production is often relatively cheaper, even though wages are high: 'On the world market the more productive national labour reckons also as the more intense ... The relative value of money will, therefore, be less in the nation with the more developed capitalist mode of production than in the nation with the less developed'.[29] In other words, high profits are perfectly compatible with high wages – and low profits with low pay.

Another argument associated with globalisation is the notion that production is most effective where it is most flexible. A range of goods can be achieved through flexible production, while the way to achieve flexible production is by reducing stocks of products and raw materials. According to the theorists of just-in-time production, even materials and machinery should be purchased according to the latest trends of demand. One way to meet the demands of the consumer is by keeping the supply of new means of production to a minimum. By contrast, in *Capital 2* (published posthumously in 1885), Karl Marx argued that the only way to achieve continuous production was through establishing a steady supply of raw materials, 'To the extent that there is no rapidity, regularity, and security of supply [of raw materials], the latent part of the productive capital in the hands of the producer, that is to say the supply of raw materials waiting to be used, must increase in size'.[30] Although it may be possible to reduce stocks of finished products, it is much harder for firms to treat raw materials in the same way.

Another of the claims associated with globalisation is the suggestion that industrial capital is becoming less important, while financial capital is now dominant. As finance has become more globalised, and it is possible to buy stocks and shares all round the world, so where finance has blazed the trail, production must follow and move in the same way. Marx argued the reverse, that under conditions of advanced capitalism, finance is subordinate to industry, and that this could be observed at times of boom and slump. The varied fortunes of international finance tended to follow the highs and lows of industrial production. 'In the preliminary stages of bourgeois society, trade dominates industry; in modern society, the opposite'.[31]

Section eight, 'Capital, finance and profit', includes a passage from Marx's *Capital 3* (published posthumously in 1894), which sketches the relationship between money capital and productive industry. There is also a passage from Marx's 1861-3 *Economic Manuscripts*, in which the author first sketched out his claim that there was a tendency for the rate of profit to decline. Marx maintained that increased spending on machinery, as opposed to labour, was in the interest of individual capitalists, but not in the interest of the system as a whole. Each time it invested in the latest means of production, one company would be able to steal a march on its rivals, but as more and more money was spent on machinery and less on labour, so the general level of investment would grow faster than value. The ratio of profit to investment would decline. The most advanced levels of production would become the norm, while the level of profits would shrink compared to costs. Costs would rise much quicker than profits. In effect, Marx argued that capitalism had a tendency to age, and would go into crisis, which is a long way from the optimistic visions of the enthusiastic globalisers.

The final section, 'Labour', sets out Karl Marx and Frederick Engels' hope that international capitalist production would meet its nemesis in an international revolt of labour. As well as supporting the demands of workers, they also called for the extension of national rights. Within the International Working Men's Association, Marx and Engels campaigned against American slavery and for the right of the oppressed Poles to form their own state. These 'bourgeois' democratic demands stood absolutely in line with their vision of a workers' revolution. They hoped that the revolution would spread, becoming more socialist as it advanced from one country to another. What began with localised campaigns against national oppression would become a popular movement with socialist goals:

> While the democratic petty bourgeoisie wish to bring the revolution to a conclusion as quickly as possible, and with the achievement, at most, of the above demands, it is our interest and our task to make the revolution permanent, until all more or less possessing classes have been forced out of their position of dominance, the proletariat has conquered state power, and the association of proletarians, not only in one country but in all the dominant countries of the world, has advanced so far that competition among the proletarians in these countries has ceased and that at least the decisive productive forces are concentrated in the hands of the proletarians.[32]

Marx and Engels believed that the workers in the richest nations could secure their liberation only if they fought together with workers in the poorest countries. Working-class politics had to be international, or it was nothing. This belief informed Marx's famous letter to Kugelmann, in which he argued that English workers must fight the oppression of the Irish, 'They will never be able to do anything decisive here in England before they separate their attitude towards Ireland quite definitely from that of the ruling classes ... And that must be done not out of a sympathy for Ireland, but as a demand based on the interests of the English proletariat'.[33] The goal of internationalism is expressed in this book by the concluding section of the *German Ideology*, in which Marx argued that the creation of big business, made possible the growth of the working-class, which was a force for change. Even though production may have diversified in recent years, capital is bigger and more centralised than ever before. There are also more workers – only in the last 20 years has the industrial proletariat outgrown the rural peasantry in global terms. In this argument, as elsewhere, Marx remains relevant today.[34]

Having summarised the contents, it is appropriate to return to the aim of this book. The hope is to remind readers of the creative and vital way in which Marx approached these questions, taking concrete examples and always engaging with the world as it was. In his lifetime, Marx supported the victims of colonialism in their uprisings against British rule, and British workers in their revolts as well. He would have had no difficulty in choosing sides between the oppressed and global capital. It is more likely, though, that Marx and Engels would have been sceptical of the theory of all-consuming globalisation. For all the current talk of global capital now being free of all constraints, it remains true that if something is to be sold then it must first be made, and that every product must have someone who produced it. Capital and labour both remain more fixed than globalisation theory would allow. In short, these extracts from Marx and Engels describe a world which was not so different from our own.

Yet the purpose of this book is not to demonstrate the truth or falsehood of the globalisation thesis. Economic theories can only be tested on the basis of evidence taken from the world economy at this moment in time. Either there is a strong trend towards the internationalisation of production, or there is not. Either flexible production is becoming dominant within manufacture, or it is not. These are questions of fact: they cannot be decided simply on the basis of a few quotations from Marx and Engels. In *The Holy Family*, Marx and Engels' critique of German left-Hegelianism, the authors joke at the mystification practised by Ludwig Feuerbach, Max Stirner and the other philosophers of this generation:

> Once upon a time a valiant fellow had the idea that men were drowned in water only because they were possessed with the *idea of gravity*. If they were to get this notion out of their heads, say by allowing it to be a superstitious, a religious concept, they would be sublimely proof against any danger from water. His whole life long he fought against the illusion of gravity, of whose harmful consequences all statistics bought him new and manifold evidence. This valiant fellow was the type of the new revolutionary philosophers in Germany.[35]

The valiant fellow is also reminiscent of certain species of 'Marxists' who would resolve the contradictions of globalisation not in reality, but in their own heads. Having chosen Marx for the open character of his work, it would be quite wrong to imagine that Marx somehow mapped out the entire laws of development for capital in his own day and for all time. For that reason, this book is necessarily provisional. Faced with the question of whether the world economy is becoming more globalised, this book may help others to contribute to an answer, it is not the answer itself.

It is also important to remember that the very meaning of the term globalisation can change with its use. In the mid-1990s, the term was synonymous with corporate power. New technology seemed to encourage the further advance of the multinationals. Yet over the past year or two, the very institutions of globalisation have come under greater scrutiny. This process began in winter 1999, with huge protests outside the meeting of the World Trade Organisation in Seattle. Since then, the IMF and World Bank have experienced similar opposition, in Washington, Millau, Kyoto, Seoul and Prague and elsewhere. One banner at Prague declared that 'Our resistance must be as global as capital'. Marxists have much to learn from this new anti-capitalist movement, while the movement itself has something to learn from Karl Marx.

For many years, Karl Marx's theories were under attack. There was no thinker in the world who was so often and so routinely dismissed as irrelevant to contemporary debate. Yet the past five years have witnessed the growth of a remarkable new interest in Marx's economic and historical work. Nearly 100,000 copies of the *Communist Manifesto* were sold in Britain between 1996 and 1997. Meanwhile, the *London Review of Books*, the *Financial Times*, the *New Yorker* have all praised Marx for his ability to make sense of the world economy.[36] With the Cold War over, readers can choose for themselves what to make of Marx and Engels' work. Karl Marx has returned, and his ideas are again open to honest debate. If this book encourages new readers to read Marx for themselves, then its purpose will have been served. Hopefully, this book will be part of a trend.

NOTES

1. Independent Commission on Population and the Quality of Life, *Caring for the Future, Making the Next Decades Provide a Life Worth Living*, Oxford University Press, Oxford and New York 1996, p47.

2. *Financial Times*, 8 May 1987; *Guardian*, 7 July 1997; N. Klein, *No Logo*, Flamingo, London 2000; G. Monbiot, *Captive State*, Fourth Estate, London 2000.

3. F. McDonagh, 'Work in a Globalised World', in D. Livingstone (ed), *Work, An Anthology* Katabasis, London 1999, pp125-143; M. Waters, *Globalisation*, Routledge, London 1995, p1; M. Walker, *The Cold War and the Making of the Modern World*, Fourth Estate, London 1993, p355.

4. M. Miyoshi, 'Sites of Resistance in the Global Economy', in *Cultural Readings of Imperialism: Edward Said and the Gravity of History*, K. Ansell-Pearson, M. Parry and J. Squires (eds), Lawrence and Wishart, London 1997, pp49-66.

5. A. Giddens, *The Consequences of Modernity*, Polity, Cambridge 1990, p64; also A. Giddens, *Beyond Left and Right: The Future of Radical Politics*, Polity, Cambridge 1994, pp292-293 and passim.

6. U. Hannerz, 'Cosmopolitans and Locals in World Culture', in *Global Culture: Nationalism, Globalisation and Modernity*, M. Featherstone (ed), Sage, London 1990.

7. J. Tomlinson, *Cultural Imperialism: A Critical Introduction*, Pinter, London 1991, p175.

8. Z. Bauman, *Work, Consumerism and the New Poor*, Open University Press, Buckingham 1998, p24.

9. J. Martin, 'The Social and the Political' in *Contemporary, Social and Political Theory*, F. Ashe et al. (eds), Open University Press, Buckingham 1999, pp155-178.

10. J. Habermas, 'The European Nation-State and the Pressures of Globalisation', *New Left Review* 235 (1999), pp46-59.

11. J. Gray, *False Dawn: The Delusions of Global Capitalism*, Granta, London 1998, p209.

12. S. Strange, 'The New World of Debt', *New Left Review* 230 (1998), pp91-114.

13. N. Harris, *The End of the Third World: Newly Industrialising Countries and the Decline of an Ideology*, Penguin, Harmondsworth 1986.

14. S. Lasch and J. Urry, *The End of Organised Capitalism*, Polity, Cambridge 1987, pp5-6; D. Coyle, *The Weightless World*, Capstone, London 1997.

15. R. J. Ross and C. Trachte, *Global Capitalism, The New Leviathan*, New York University Press, New York 1990, p3.

16. K. Moody, *Workers in a Lean World*, Verso, London and New York 1997,

p113; A. Budd, 'Workers in a Lean World', *Historical Materialism* 3 (1998), pp189-201.

17. P. Hirst and G. Thompson, *Globalization in Question*, Polity, Cambridge 1996; there are also sceptical perspectives in R. Kiely and P. Marfleet, *Globalisation and the Third World*, Routledge, London 1998; and C. Harman, 'Globalisation, A Critique of a new Orthodoxy, *International Socialism Journal* 73 (1997), pp3-34.

18. E. Hobsbawm, 'Introduction', in K. Marx and F. Engels, *Communist Manifesto*, Verso, New York and London 1998 edn, pp1-30, 17.

19. The quotation from Marx and Engels' *Communist Manifesto*, is taken from extract 1, below. For the World Bank report, Moody, *Workers in a Lean World, op. cit.,* pp43-44.

20. Extract 2, below.

21. K. Popper, *The Open Society and its Enemies*, Routledge and Kegan Paul, London 1957 edn; this approach is criticised in A. Callinicos, *Theories and Narratives: Reflections on the Philosophy of History*, Cambridge, Polity 1995, pp78-81.

22. Karl Marx and Frederick Engels, *Collected Works*, hereafter *MECW*, Lawrence and Wishart, London various dates, vol. 35, p9.

23. Extract 6, below.

24. P. Anderson, *Lineages of the Absolutist State*, Verso, London 1979 edn, p488; see also L. Trotsky, *The History of the Russian Revolution*, M. Eastman (trans), Pluto, London 1977 edn, pp28-38.

25. Extract 8, below.

26. Extract 10, below. For Said's critique of Marx, E. W. Said, *Orientalism*, Routledge and Kegan Paul, London and Henley 1978, pp153-6.

27. Extract 11, below.

28. Extracts 13-15, below.

29. Extract 17, below.

30. Extract 18, below.

31. K. Marx, *Grundrisse*, New Left Books, London 1973 edn, p856.

32. *MECW* 10, p281.

33. *MECW* 24, pp55-58.

34. Extract 21, below.

35. *MECW* 5, p24.

36. J. Rees, 'The Return of Marx', *International Socialism Journal* 79 (1998), pp3-11; S. Holmes, 'The End of Idiocy on a Planetary Scale', *London Review of Books*, 29 October 1998; *Marxism Today*, special issue, October 1998; P Aspden, 'The Place where all Workers are United', *Financial Times*, 28-9 March 1998; J. Cassiday, 'The Next Great Thinker, the Return of Karl Marx', *The New Yorker*, 20-27 October 1998.

Section 1: The world economy

1. Karl Marx and Frederick Engels, 'Bourgeois and Proletarians', from *The Communist Manifesto* (1848), *Marx and Engels Collected Works*, vol. 6, pp483-96

People who have never read Marx or Engels assume that their attitude towards the development of capitalism was simply negative. In fact, their response was more complex. Growing up in early nineteenth-century Germany, both Marx and Engels saw around them societies still shaped by the long development of previous modes of production. In contrast to the rural, deferential world of feudalism, capitalism was both dynamic and new. *The Communist Manifesto*, their best known work, celebrated this increase in the human capacity to transform the world. Marx and Engels wrote of the destruction of old ideas, of ways of living which had lasted for hundreds of years. They described the 'wonders' of capitalism, far surpassing the wonders of the ancient world. Their awe was real.

Just as people today are astonished by the giddy whirl of globalisation, so were Marx and Engels in the 1840s. In their words, 'The bourgeoisie has through its exploitation of the world market given a cosmopolitan character to production and consumption in every country ... All old-established national industries have grown or are daily being destroyed. They are dislodged by new industries ... whose products are consumed, not only at home but in every corner of the globe'.

Marx and Engels praised the bourgeoisie, the class associated with the rise of capitalist system, for its revolutionary conduct. Then with the same passion they condemned this group. Under capitalism, poverty and inequality had become ever more widespread. What was required instead was a society which took the machines, and used them for human ends. A communist world would use the wealth generated under capitalism, and distribute it equally, from each according to their ability, to each according to their need.

1

BOURGEOIS AND PROLETARIANS[1]

The history of all hitherto existing society[2] is the history of class struggles.

Freeman and slave, patrician and plebeian, lord and serf, guild-master[3] and journeyman, in a word, oppressor and oppressed, stood in constant opposition to one another, carried on an uninterrupted, now hidden, now open fight, a fight that each time ended, either in a revolutionary re-constitution of society, at large, or in the common ruin of the contending classes.

In the earlier epochs of history, we find almost everywhere a complicated arrangement of society into various orders, a manifold gradation of social rank. In ancient Rome we have patricians, knights, plebeians, slaves; in the Middle Ages, feudal lords, guild-masters, journeymen, apprentices, serfs; in almost all of classes, again, subordinate gradations.

The modern bourgeois society that has sprouted from the ruins of feudal society has not done away with class antagonisms. It has but established new classes, new conditions of oppression, new forms of struggle in place of the old ones.

Our epoch, the epoch of the bourgeoisie, possesses, however, this distinctive feature: it has simplified the class antagonisms. Society as a whole is more and more splitting up into two great hostile camps, into two great classes directly facing each other: Bourgeoisie and Proletariat.

From the serfs of the Middle Ages sprang the chartered burghers of the earliest towns. From these burgesses the first elements of the bourgeoisie were developed.

The discovery of America, the rounding of the Cape, opened up fresh ground for the rising bourgeoisie. The East-Indian and Chinese markets, the colonisation of America, trade with the colonies, the increase in the means of exchange and in commodities generally, gave to commerce, to navigation, to industry, an impulse never before known, and thereby, to the revolutionary element in the tottering feudal society, a rapid development.

The feudal system of industry, under which industrial production was monopolised by closed guilds, now no longer sufficed for the growing wants of the new markets. The manufacturing system took its place. The guild-masters were pushed on one side by the manufacturing middle class; division of labour between the different corporate guilds vanished in the face of division of labour in each single workshop.

Meantime the markets kept ever growing, the demand ever rising. Even manufacture no longer sufficed. Thereupon, steam and machinery revolutionised industrial production. The place of manufacture was taken by the giant, Modern Industry, the place of the industrial middle class, by industrial millionaires, the leaders of whole industrial armies, the modern bourgeois.

Modern industry has established the world market, for which the discovery of America paved the way. This market has given an immense development to commerce, to navigation, to communication by land. This development has, in its turn, reacted on the extension of industry; and in proportion as industry, commerce, navigation, railways extended, in the same proportion the bourgeoisie developed, increased its capital, and pushed into the background every class handed down from the Middle Ages.

We see, therefore, how the modern bourgeoisie is itself the product of a long course of development, of a series of revolutions in the modes of production and of exchange.

Each step in the development of the bourgeoisie was accompanied by a corresponding political advance of that class. An oppressed class under the sway of the feudal nobility, an armed and self-governing association in the medieval commune;[4] here independent urban republic (as in Italy and Germany), there taxable 'third estate' of the monarchy (as in France), afterwards, in the period of manufacture proper, serving either the semi-feudal or the absolute monarchy as a counterpoise against the nobility, and, in fact, cornerstone of the great monarchies in general, the bourgeoisie has at last, since the establishment of Modern Industry, and of the world market, conquered for itself, in the modern representative State, exclusive political sway. The executive of the modern State is but a committee for managing the common affairs of the whole bourgeoisie.

The bourgeoisie, historically, has played a most revolutionary part.

The bourgeoisie, wherever it has got the upper hand, has put an end to all feudal, patriarchal, idyllic relations. It has pitilessly torn asunder the motley feudal ties that bound man to his 'natural superiors', and has left remaining no other nexus between mail and man than naked self-interest, than callous 'cash payment'. It has drowned the most heavenly ecstasies of religious fervour, of chivalrous enthusiasm, of philistine sentimentalism, in the icy water of egotistical calculation. It has resolved personal worth into exchange value, and in place of the numberless indefeasible chartered freedoms, has set up that single, unconscionable freedom – Free Trade. In one word, for exploitation, veiled by religious and political illusions, it has substituted naked, shameless, direct, brutal exploitation.

The bourgeoisie has stripped of its halo every occupation hitherto honoured and looked up to with reverent awe. It has converted the physician, the lawyer, the priest, the poet, the man of science, into its paid wage-labourers.

The bourgeoisie has torn away from the family its sentimental veil, and has reduced the family relation to a mere money relation.

The bourgeoisie has disclosed how it came to pass that the brutal display of vigour in the Middle Ages, which Reactionists so much admire, found its fitting complement in the most slothful indolence. It has been the first to show what man's activity can bring about. It has accomplished wonders far surpassing Egyptian pyramids, Roman aqueducts, and Gothic cathedrals; it has conducted expeditions that put in the shade all former Exoduses of nations and crusades.

The bourgeoisie cannot exist without constantly revolutionising the instruments of production, and thereby the relations of production, and with them the whole relations of society. Conservation of the old modes of production in unaltered form, was, on the contrary, the first condition of existence for all earlier industrial classes. Constant revolutionising of production, uninterrupted disturbance of all social conditions, everlasting uncertainty and agitation distinguish the bourgeois epoch from all earlier ones. All fixed, fast-frozen relations, with their train of ancient and venerable prejudices and opinions, are swept away, all new-formed ones become antiquated before they can ossify. All that is solid melts into air, all that is holy is profaned, and man is at last compelled to face with sober senses, his real conditions of life, and his relations with his kind.

The need of a constantly expanding market for its products chases the bourgeoisie over the whole surface of the globe. It must nestle everywhere, settle everywhere, establish connexions everywhere.

The bourgeoisie has through its exploitation of the world market given a cosmopolitan character to production and consumption in every country. To the great chagrin of Reactionists, it has drawn from under the feet of industry the national ground on which it stood. All old-established national industries have been destroyed or are daily, being destroyed. They are dislodged by new industries, whose introduction becomes a life and death question for all civilised nations, by industries that no longer work up indigenous raw material, but raw material drawn from the remotest zones; industries whose products are consumed, not only at home, but in every quarter of the globe. In place of the old wants, satisfied by the productions of the country, we find new wants, requiring for their satisfaction the products of distant lands and climes. In place of the old local and national seclusion and self-sufficiency, we have intercourse in every direction, universal inter-dependence of nations. And as in material, so also in intellectual production. The intellectual creations of individual nations become common property. National one-sidedness and narrow-mindedness become more and more impossible, and from the numerous national and local literatures, there arises a world literature.

The bourgeoisie, by the rapid improvement of all instruments of production, by the immensely facilitated means of communication, draws all, even the most barbarian, nations into civilisation. The cheap prices of its commodities are the heavy artillery with which it batters down all Chinese walls, with which it forces the barbarians' intensely obstinate hatred of foreigners to capitulate. It compels all nations, on pain of extinction, to adopt the bourgeois mode of production; it compels them to introduce what it calls civilisation into their midst, i.e. to become bourgeois themselves. In one word, it creates a world after its own image.

The bourgeoisie has subjected the country to the rule of the towns. It has enormous cities, has greatly increased the urban population as compared with the rural, and has thus rescued a considerable part of the population from the idiocy of rural life. Just as it has made the country dependent on the towns, so it has made barbarian and semi-barbarian countries dependent on the civilised ones, nations of peasants on nations of bourgeois, the East on the West.

The bourgeoisie keeps more and more doing away with the scattered state of the population, of the means of production, and of property. It has agglomerated population, centralised means of production, and has concentrated property in a few hands. The necessary consequence of this was political centralisation. Independent, or but loosely connected provinces with separate interests, laws, governments and systems of taxation, became lumped together into one nation, with one government, one code of laws, one national class-interest, one frontier and one customs-tariff.

The bourgeoisie, during its rule of scarce one hundred years, has created more massive and more colossal productive forces than have all preceding generations together. Subjection of Nature's forces to man, machinery, application of chemistry to industry and agriculture, steam-navigation, railways, electric telegraphs, clearing of whole continents for cultivation, canalisation of rivers, whole populations conjured out of the ground – what earlier century had even a presentiment that such productive forces slumbered in the lap of social labour?

We see then: the means of production and of exchange, on whose foundation the bourgeoisie built itself up, were generated in feudal society. At a certain stage in the development of these means of production and of exchange, the conditions under which feudal society produced and exchanged, the feudal organisation of agriculture and manufacturing industry, in one word, the feudal relations of property became no longer compatible with the already developed productive forces; they became so many fetters. They had to be burst asunder; they were burst asunder.

Into their place stepped free competition, accompanied by a social and political constitution adapted to it, and by the economical and political sway of the bourgeois class.

A similar movement is going on before our own eyes. Modern bourgeois society with its relations of production, of exchange and of property, a society that has conjured up such gigantic means of production and of exchange, is like the sorcerer, who is no longer able to control the powers of the nether world whom he has called up by his spells. For many a decade past the history of industry and commerce is but the history of the revolt of modern productive forces against modern conditions of production, against the property, relations that are the conditions for the existence of the bourgeoisie and of its rule. It is enough to mention the commercial crises that by their periodical return put on its trial, each time more threateningly, the existence of the entire bourgeois society. In these crises a great part not only of the existing products, but also of the previously created productive forces, are periodically destroyed. In these crises there breaks out an epidemic that, in all earlier epochs, would have seemed an absurdity – the epidemic of over-production. Society suddenly finds itself put back into a state of momentary barbarism; it appears as if a famine, a universal war of devastation had cut off the supply of every means of subsistence; industry and commerce seem to be destroyed; and why? Because there is too much civilisation, too much means of subsistence, too much industry, too much commerce. The productive forces at the disposal of society no longer tend to further the development of the conditions of bourgeois property; on the contrary, they have become too powerful for these conditions, by which they are fettered, and so soon as they overcome these fetters, they bring disorder into the whole of bourgeois society, endanger the existence of bourgeois property. The conditions of bourgeois society are too narrow to comprise the wealth created by them. And how does the bourgeoisie get over these crises? On the one hand by enforced destruction of a mass of forces; on the other, by the conquest of new markets, and by the more thorough exploitation of the old ones. That is to say, by paving the way for more extensive and more destructive crises, and by diminishing the means whereby crises are prevented.

The weapons with which the bourgeoisie felled feudalism to the ground are now turned against the bourgeoisie itself.

But not only has the bourgeoisie forged the weapons that bring death to itself; it has also called into existence the men who are to wield those weapons – the modern working class – the proletarians.

In proportion as the bourgeoisie, *i.e.*, capital, is developed, in the same proportion is the proletariat, the modern working class, developed – a class of labourers, who live only so long as they find work, and who finds work only so long as their labour increases capital. These labourers, who must sell themselves piecemeal, are a commodity, like every other article of commerce, and are consequently exposed to all the vicissitudes of competition, to all the fluctuations of the market.

Owing to the extensive use of machinery and to division of labour, the work of the proletarians has lost all individual character, and, consequently, all charm for the workman. He becomes an appendage of the machine, and it is only the most simple, most monotonous, and most easily, acquired knack, that is required of him. Hence, the cost of production of a workman is restricted, almost entirely, to the means of subsistence that he requires for his maintenance, and for the propagation of his race. But the price of a commodity, and therefore also of labour, is equal to its cost of production. In proportion, therefore, as the repulsiveness of the work increases, the wage decreases. Nay more, in proportion as the use of machinery and division of labour increases, in the same proportion the burden of toil also increases, whether by prolongation of the working hours, by increase of the work exacted in a given time or by increased speed of the machinery, etc.

Modern industry has converted the little workshop of the patriarchal master into the great factory of the industrial capitalist. Masses of
labourers, crowded into the factory, are organised like soldiers. As
privates of the industrial army they are placed under the command of
a perfect hierarchy of officers and sergeants. Not only are they slaves
of the bourgeois class, and of the bourgeois State; they are daily and
hourly enslaved by the machine, by the overlooker, and, above all, by
the individual bourgeois manufacturer himself. The more openly this
despotism proclaims gain to be its end and aim, the more petty, the
more hateful and the more embittering it is.

The less the skill and exertion of strength implied in manual labour,
in other words, the more modern industry becomes developed, the
more is the labour of men superseded by that of women. Differences of
age and sex have no longer any distinctive social validity for the working class. All are instruments of labour, more or less expensive to use,
according to their age and sex.

No sooner is the exploitation of the labourer by the manufacturer,
so far, at an end, and he receives his wages in cash, than he is set upon
by the other portions of the bourgeoisie, the landlord, the shopkeeper,
the pawnbroker, etc.

The lower strata of the middle class – the small tradespeople, shop-
keepers, and retired tradesmen generally, the handicraftsmen and
peasants – all these sink gradually into the proletariat, partly because
their diminutive capital does not suffice for the scale on which Modern
Industry is carried on, and is swamped in the competition with the
large capitalists, partly because their specialised skill is rendered worth-
less by new methods of production. Thus the proletariat is recruited
from all classes of the population.

The proletariat goes through various stages of development. With its
birth begins its struggle with the bourgeoisie. At first the contest is
carried on by individual labourers, then by the workpeople of a
factory, then by the operatives of one trade, in one locality, against the
individual bourgeois who directly, exploits them. They direct their
attacks not against the bourgeois conditions of production, but against
the instruments of production themselves; they destroy imported

wares that compete with their labour, they smash to pieces machinery, they set factories ablaze, they seek to restore by force the vanished status of the workman of the Middle Ages.

At this stage the labourers still form an incoherent mass scattered over the whole country, and broken up by, their mutual competition. If anywhere they unite to form more compact bodies, this is not yet the consequence of their own active union, but of the union of the bourgeoisie, which class, in order to attain its own political ends, is compelled to set the whole proletariat in motion, and is moreover yet, for a time able to do so. At this stage, therefore, the proletarians do not fight their enemies, but the enemies of their enemies, the remnants of absolute monarchy, the landowners, the non-industrial bourgeois, the petty bourgeoisie. Thus the whole historical movement is concentrated in the hands of the bourgeoisie; every victory so obtained is a victory for the bourgeoisie.

But with the development of industry the proletariat not only increases in number; it becomes concentrated in greater masses, its strength grows, and it feels that strength more. The various interests and conditions of life within the ranks of the proletariat are more and more equalised, in proportion as machinery obliterates all distinctions of labour, and nearly everywhere reduces wages to the same low level. The growing competition among the bourgeois, and the resulting commercial crises, make the wages of the workers ever more rapidly developing, makes their livelihood more and more precarious; the collisions between individual workmen and individual bourgeois take more and more the character of collisions between two classes. Thereupon the workers begin to form combinations (Trades' Unions) against the bourgeois; they club together in order to keep up the rate of wages; they found permanent associations in order to make provision beforehand for these occasional revolts. Here and there the contest breaks out into riots.

Now and then the workers are victorious, but only for a time. The real fruit of their battles lies, not in the immediate result, but in the ever-expanding union of the workers. This union is helped on by the improved means of communication that are created by modern industry and that place the workers of different localities in contact with one another. It was just this contact that was needed to centralise the numerous local struggles, all of the same character, into one national struggle between classes. But every class struggle is a political struggle. And that union, to attain which the burghers of the Middle Ages, with their miserable highways, required centuries, the modern proletarians, thanks to the railways, achieve in a few years.

This organisation of the proletarians into a class, and consequently into a political party, is continually being upset again by the competition between the workers themselves. But it ever rises up again, stronger, firmer, mightier. It compels legislative recognition of particular interests of the workers, by taking advantage of the divisions among the bourgeoisie itself. Thus the ten-hours' bill in England was carried.

Altogether collisions between the classes of the old society further, in many ways, the course of development of the proletariat. The bourgeoisie finds itself involved in a constant battle. At first with the aristocracy; later on, with those portions of the bourgeoisie itself, whose interests have become antagonistic to the progress of industry; at all times, with the bourgeoisie of foreign countries. In all these battles it sees itself compelled to appeal to the proletariat, to ask for its help, and thus, to drag it into the political arena. The bourgeoisie itself, therefore, supplies the proletariat with its own elements of political and general education, in other words, it furnishes the proletariat with weapons for fighting the bourgeoisie.

Further, as we have already seen, entire sections of the ruling classes are, by the advance of industry, precipitated into the proletariat, or are at least threatened in their conditions of existence. These also supply the proletariat with fresh elements of enlightenment and progress.

Finally, in times when the class struggle nears the decisive hour, the process of dissolution going on within the ruling class, in fact within the whole range of old society, assumes such a violent, glaring character, that a small section of the ruling class cuts itself adrift, and joins the revolutionary class, the class that holds the future in its hands. Just as, therefore, at an earlier period, a section of the nobility went over to the bourgeoisie, so now a portion of the bourgeoisie goes over to the proletariat, and in particular, a portion of the bourgeois ideologists, who have raised themselves to the level of comprehending theoretically the historical movement as a whole.

Of all the classes that stand face to face with the bourgeoisie today, the proletariat alone is a really revolutionary class. The other classes decay and finally disappear in the face of Modern Industry; the proletariat is its special and essential product.

The lower middle class, the small manufacturer, the shopkeeper, the artisan, the peasant, all these fight against the bourgeoisie, to save from extinction their existence as fractions of the middle class. They are therefore not revolutionary, but conservative. Nay more, they are reactionary, for they try to roll back the wheel of history. If by chance they are revolutionary, they are so only in view of their impending transfer into the proletariat, they thus defend not their present, but their future interests, they desert their own standpoint to place themselves at that of the proletariat.

The 'dangerous class', the social scum[5], that passively rotting mass thrown off by the lowest layers of old society may, here and there, be swept into the movement by a proletarian revolution; its conditions of life, however, prepare it far more for the part of a bribed tool of reactionary intrigue.

In the conditions of the proletariat, those of the old society at large are already virtually swamped. The proletarian is without property; his relation to his wife and children has no longer anything in common with the bourgeois family relations; modern industrial labour, modern subjection to capital, the same in England as in France, in America as in Germany, has stripped him of every trace of national character. Law, morality, religion, are to him so many bourgeois prejudices, behind which lurk in ambush just as many bourgeois interests.

All the preceding classes that got the upper hand, sought to fortify their already acquired status by subjecting society at large to their conditions of appropriation. The proletarians cannot become masters of the productive forces of society, except by abolishing their own previous mode of appropriation, and thereby also every other previous mode of appropriation. They have nothing of their own to secure and to fortify; their mission is to destroy all previous securities for, and insurances of, individual property.

All previous historical movements were movements of minorities, or in the interest of minorities. The proletarian movement is the self-conscious, independent movement of the immense majority, in the interest of the immense majority. The proletariat, the lowest stratum of our present society, cannot stir, cannot raise itself up, without the whole superincumbent strata of official society being sprung into the air.

Though not in substance, yet in form, the struggle of the proletariat with the bourgeoisie is at first a national struggle. The proletariat of each country must, of course, first of all settle matters with its own bourgeoisie.

In depicting the most general phases of the development of the proletariat, we traced the more or less veiled civil war, raging within existing society, up to the point where that war breaks out into open revolution, and where the violent overthrow of the bourgeoisie lays the foundation for the sway of the proletariat.

Hitherto, every form of society has been based, as we have already seen, on the antagonism of oppressing and oppressed classes. But in order to oppress a class, certain conditions must be assured to it under which it can, at least, continue its slavish existence. The serf, in the period of serfdom, raised himself to membership in the commune, just as the petty bourgeois, under the yoke of feudal absolutism, managed to develop into a bourgeois. The modern labourer, on the contrary, instead of rising with the progress of industry, sinks deeper and deeper below the conditions of existence of his own class. He becomes a pauper, and pauperism develops more rapidly than population and wealth. And here it becomes evident, that the bourgeoisie is unfit any longer to be the ruling class in society, and to impose its conditions of existence upon society as an over-riding law. It is unfit to rule because it is incompetent to assure an existence to its slave within his slavery, because it cannot help letting him sink into such a state, that it has to feed him, instead of being fed by him. Society can no longer live under this bourgeoisie, in other words, its existence is no longer compatible with society.

The essential condition for the existence, and for the sway of the bourgeois class, is the formation and augmentation of capital; the condition for capital is wage-labour. Wage-labour rests exclusively on competition between the labourers. The advance of industry, whose involuntary promoter is the bourgeoisie, replaces the isolation of the labourers, due to competition, by their revolutionary combination, due to association. The development of Modern Industry, therefore, cuts from under its feet the very foundation on which the bourgeoisie produces and appropriates products. What the bourgeoisie, therefore, produces, above all, is its own grave-diggers. Its fall and the victory of the proletariat are equally inevitable.

NOTES

1. By bourgeoisie is meant the class of modern Capitalists, owners of the means of social production and employers of wage-labour. By proletariat, the class of modern wage-labourers who, having no means of production of their own, are reduced to selling their labour-power in order to live. [*Note by Engels to the English edition of 1888.*]
2. That is, all *written* history. In 1847, the pre-history of society, the social organisation existing previous to recorded history, was all but unknown. Since then, Haxthausen discovered common ownership of land in Russia. Maurer proved it to be the social foundation from which all Teutonic races started in history, and by and by village communities were found to be, or to have been the primitive form of society everywhere from India to Ireland. The inner organisation of this primitive Communist society was laid bare, in its typical form, by Morgan's crowning discovery of the true nature of the *gens* and its relation to the *tribe*. With the dissolution of these primeval communities society begins to be differentiated into deparate and finally antagonistic classes. I have attempted to retrace this process of dissolution in *Der Ursprung der Familie, des Privateigenthums und des Staats*, 2nd edition, Stuttgart, 1886. [*Note by Engels to the English edition of 1888, and – less the last sentence – to the German edition of 1890.*]
3. Guild-master, that is, a full member of a guild, a master within, not a head of a guild. [*Note by Engels to the English edition of 1888.*]
4. 'Commune' was the name taken, in France, by the nascent towns even before they had conquered from their feudal lords and masters of local self-government and political rights as the 'Third Estate'. Generally speaking, for the economical development of the bourgeoisie. England is here taken as the typical country; for its political development, France. [*Note by Engels to the English edition of 1888.*]

This was the name given to their urban communities by the townsmen of Italy and France, after they had purchased or wrested their initial rights of self-government from their feudal lords. [*Note by Engels to the English edition of 1890.*]

5. The German editions have 'lumpen proletariat' instead of 'the dangerous class, the social scum'. [*Ed.*]

Section 2: Progress

2. Frederick Engels, 'Outlines of a Critique of Political Economy' (1844), *Marx and Engels Collected Works*, vol. 3, pp422-424

3. Karl Marx, 'Speech on Free Trade' (1847), *Marx and Engels Collected Works*, vol. 6, pp287-290

4. Karl Marx, 'Genesis of the Industrial Capitalist', from *Capital 1* (1867), *Marx and Engels Collected Works*, vol. 35, pp738-748

5. Frederick Engels, 'England in 1845 and 1885' (1885), *Marx and Engels Collected Works*, vol. 26, pp298-301

Marx and Engels wrote these four extracts over a forty-year period. Each deals with the theme of progress. According to the dominant liberal ideas of the day, all future developments were changes for the better. Facts were superior to ignorance, production better than indolence, and the world-market was the highest form of civilisation known to man. The inheritors of this argument can be found today defending globalisation. Their argument is simple – if globalisation is the future, then this must be the only way in which things could go. In contrast to this liberal idea of progress, Karl Marx and Frederick Engels maintained that the rise of capitalism was contradictory. On the one hand, capitalism brought with it enormous human suffering. On the other hand, the spread of knowledge, technique and industry increased the possibilities for a different, and democratically-run society to emerge.

The first extract is a preliminary sketch on economics – written by Engels when he was just twenty-three. Some formulations are unfinished, but the passage is included for its passionate attack on economic 'liberalism'. While liberal theorists maintained that the progress of trade would lead to a new world of human freedom, in practice a new tyranny was created. The second extract, Karl Marx's 'Speech on Free Trade', was concerned with the argument for trade liberalisation or tariffs (protectionism), which dominated British political life at this time. Marx, of course, regarded freed trade as a sham – the surprising theme of this passage is his opposition to protectionism, as well. Karl Marx had hoped to deliver the speech at a large Brussels conference on the subject, but was prevented from speaking, and only Engels' diligence saved the speech to be recorded in print.

The third extract is taken from *Capital*, volume I. This was initially conceived by Marx as a six-volume publication, which would cover every aspect of the world economy, including Capital, Landed Property, Wage Labour, The State, International Trade, and the World Market. Yet only the first volume of the first part was published in Marx's lifetime. This historical passage details the enormous concentration of wealth through slavery and empire which enabled later advances towards industrialisation to take place. In Marx's words, capitalism came into the world 'dripping with blood and dirt'. The fourth extract is from a late piece by Engels, looking back on forty years of England's economic ascendancy. Frederick Engels emphasises here the need for capital to expand. What would happen once the dominant power of the time started to lose its grip? Forty years on from his first arrival in England, Engels observed that the optimism associated with free trade was already lost. The international system of commodity exchange had undermined the fortunes even of the greatest trading power of the day.

2

OUTLINES OF A CRITIQUE OF POLITICAL ECONOMY

The immediate consequence of private property is *trade* – exchange of reciprocal requirements – buying and selling. This trade, like every activity, must under the dominion of private property become a direct source of gain for the trader; i.e. each must seek to sell as dear as possible and buy as cheap as possible. In every purchase and sale, therefore, two men with diametrically opposed interests confront each other. The confrontation is decidedly antagonistic, for each knows the intentions of the other – knows that they are opposed to his own. Therefore, the first consequence is mutual mistrust, on the one hand, and the justification of this mistrust – the application of immoral means to attain an immoral end – on the other. Thus, the first maxim in trade is secretiveness – the concealment of everything which might reduce the value of the article in question. The result is that in trade it is permitted to take the utmost advantage of the ignorance, the trust, of the opposing party, and likewise to impute qualities to one's commodity which it does not possess. In a word, trade is legalised fraud. Any merchant who wants to give truth its due can bear me witness that actual practice conforms with this theory.

The mercantile system still had a certain artless Catholic candour and did not in the least conceal the immoral nature of trade. We have seen how it openly paraded its mean avarice. The mutually hostile attitude of the nations in the eighteenth century, loathsome envy and trade jealousy, were the logical consequences of trade as such. Public opinion had not yet become humanised. Why, therefore, conceal things which resulted from the inhuman, hostile nature of trade itself?

But when the *economic Luther*, Adam Smith, criticised past economics things had changed considerably.[1] The century had been humanised; reason had asserted itself; morality began to claim its eternal right. The extorted trade treaties, the commercial wars, the strict isolation of the nations, offended too greatly against advanced consciousness. Protestant hypocrisy took the place of Catholic candour. Smith proved that humanity, too, was rooted in the nature of commerce; that commerce must become 'among nations, as among individuals, a bond of union and friendship' instead of being 'the most fertile source of discord and animosity' (cf. *Wealth of Nations*, Bk. 4, Ch. 3, Section 2); that after all it lay in the nature of things for trade, taken overall, to be advantageous to *all* parties concerned.

Smith was right to eulogise trade as humane. There is nothing absolutely immoral in the world. Trade, too, has an aspect wherein it pays homage to morality and humanity. But what homage! The law of the strong hand, the open highway robbery of the Middle Ages, became humanised when it passed over into trade; and trade became humanised when its first stage characterised by the prohibition of the export of money passed over into the mercantile system. Then the mercantile system itself was humanised. Naturally, it is in the interest of the trader to be on good terms with the one from whom he buys cheap as well as with the other to whom he sells dear. A nation therefore acts very imprudently if it fosters feelings of animosity in its suppliers and customers. The more friendly, the more advantageous. Such is the humanity of trade. And this hypocritical way of misusing morality for immoral purposes is the pride of the free-trade system. 'Have we not overthrown the barbarism of the monopolies?' exclaim the hypocrites. 'Have we not brought about the fraternisation of the peoples, and reduced the number of wars?' Yes, all this you have done – but *how*! You have destroyed the small monopolies so that the *one* great basic monopoly, property, may function the more freely and unrestrictedly. You have civilised the ends of the earth to win new terrain for the development of your vile avarice. You have brought about the fraternisation of the peoples – but the fraternity is the fraternity of thieves. You have reduced the number of wars – to earn all the bigger profits in peace, to intensify to the utmost the enmity between individuals, the ignominious war of competition! When have you done anything out of pure humanity, from consciousness of the futility of the opposition between the general and the individual interest? When have you been moral without being interested, without harbouring at the back of your mind immoral, egoistical motives?

By dissolving nationalities, the liberal economic system had done its best to universalise enmity, to transform mankind into a horde of ravenous beasts (for what else are competitors?) who devour one another just *because* each has identical interests with all the others – after this preparatory work there remained but one step to take before the goal was reached, the dissolution of the family. To accomplish this, economy's own beautiful invention, the factory system, came to its aid. The last vestige of common interests, the community of goods in the possession of the family, has been undermined by the factory system and – at least here in England – is already in the process of dissolution. It is a common practice for children, as soon as they are capable of work (i.e., as soon as they reach the age of nine), to spend their wages themselves, to look upon their parental home as a mere boarding-house, and hand over to their parents a fixed amount for food and lodging. How can it be otherwise? What else can result from the separation of interests, such as forms the basis of the free-trade system? Once a principle is set in motion, it works by its own impetus through all its consequences, whether the economists like it or not.

But the economist does not know himself what cause he serves. He does not know that with all his egoistical reasoning he nevertheless forms but a link in the chain of mankind's universal progress. He does not know that by his dissolution of all sectional interests he merely paves the way for the great transformation to which the century is moving – the reconciliation of mankind with nature and with itself.

NOTE

1. Cf. Karl Marx, *Economic and Philosophic Manuscripts of 1844*, in *MECW* vol. 3, Lawrence and Wishart, London 1975. [*Ed.*]

3

SPEECH OF DR MARX ON PROTECTION, FREE TRADE, AND THE WORKING CLASSES

There are two sects of protectionists. The first sect, represented in Germany by Dr List, who never intended to protect manual labour, on the contrary, they demanded protective duties in order to crush manual labour by machinery, to supersede patriarchal manufacture by modern manufacture. They always intended to prepare the reign of the monied classes (the *bourgeoisie*), and more particularly that of the large manufacturing capitalists. They openly proclaimed the ruin of petty manufacturers, of small tradesmen, and small farmers, as an event to be regretted, indeed, but quite inevitable, at the same time. The second school of protectionists, required not only protection, but absolute prohibition. They proposed to protect manual labour against the invasion of machinery, as well as against foreign competition. They proposed to protect by high duties, not only home manufacturers, but also home agriculture, and the production of raw materials at home. And where did this school arrive at? At the prohibition, not only of the importation of foreign manufactured produce, but of the progress of the home manufacture itself. Thus the whole protective system inevitably got upon the horns of this dilemma. Either it protected the progress of home manufactures, and then it sacrificed manual labour, or it protected manual labour, and then it sacrificed home manufactures. Protectionists of the first sect, those who conceived the progress of machinery, of division of labour, and of competition, to be irresistible, told the working classes, 'At any rate if you are to be squeezed out, you had better be squeezed by your own countrymen, than by foreigners'. Will the working classes for ever bear with this? I think not. Those who produce all the wealth and comforts of the rich, will not be satisfied with that poor consolation. They will require more substantial comforts in exchange for substantial produce. But the protectionists say, 'After all, we keep up the state of society as it is at present. We ensure to the working man, somehow or other, the employment he wants. We take care that he shall not be turned out of work in consequence of foreign competition'. So be it. Thus, in the best case, the protectionists avow that they are unable to arrive at anything better than the continuation of the status quo. Now the working classes want not the continuation of their actual condition, but a change for the better. A last refuge yet stands open to the protectionist. He will say that he is not at all adverse to social reform in the interior of a country, but that the first thing to ensure their success will be to shut out any derangement which might be caused by foreign competition. 'My system', he says, 'is no system of social reform, but if we are to reform society, had we not better do so within our own country, before we talk about reforms in our relations with other countries?' Very specious, indeed, but under this plausible appearance, there is hid a very strange contradiction. The protectionist system, while it gives arms to the capital of a country against the capital of foreign countries, while it strengthens capital against foreigners, believes that this capital, thus armed, thus strengthened, will be weak, impotent, and feeble, when opposed to labour. Why, that would be appealing to the mercy of capital, as if capital, considered as such, could ever be merciful. Why, social reforms are never carried by the weakness of the strong, but always by the strength of the weak. But it is not at all necessary to insist on this point. From the moment the protectionists agree that social reforms do not necessarily follow from, and that they are not part and parcel of their system, but form quite a distinct question, from that moment they abandon the question, which we discuss. We may, therefore, leave them in order to review the effects of Free Trade upon the condition of the working classes. The problem: What will be the influence of the perfect unfettering of trade upon the situation of the working classes, is very easy to be resolved. It is not even a problem. If there is anything clearly exposed in political economy, it is the fate attending the working classes under the reign of Free Trade. All those laws developed in the classical works on political economy, are strictly true under the supposition only, that trade be delivered from all fetters, that competition be perfectly free, not only within a single country, but upon the whole face of the earth. These laws, which A. Smith, Say, and Ricardo have developed, the laws under which wealth is produced and distributed – these laws grow more true, more exact, then cease to be mere abstractions, in the same measure in which Free Trade is carried out. And the master of the science, when treating of any economical subject, tells us every moment that all their reasonings are founded upon the supposition that all fetters, yet existing, are to be removed from trade. They are quite right in following this method. For they make no arbitrary abstractions, they only remove from their reasoning a series of accidental circumstances. Thus it can justly be said, that the economists – Ricardo and others – know more about society as it will be, than about society as it is. They know more about the future than about the present. If you wish to read in the book of the future, open Smith, Say, Ricardo. There you will find described, as clearly as possible, the condition which awaits the working man under the reign of perfect Free Trade. Take, for instance, the authority of Ricardo, authority than which there is no better. What is the natural normal price of the labour of, economically speaking, a working man? Ricardo replies, 'Wages reduced to their minimum – their lowest level'. Labour is a commodity as well as any other commodity. Now the price of a commodity is determined by the time necessary to produce it. What then is necessary to produce the commodity of labour? Exactly that which is necessary to produce the sum of commodities indispensable to the sustenance and the repairing of the wear and tear of the labourer, to enable him to live and to propagate, somehow or other, his race. We are, however, not to believe that the working man will never be elevated above this lowest level, nor that he never will be depressed below it. No, according to this law, the working classes will be for a time more happy, they will have for a time more than the minimum, but this surplus will be the supplement only for what they will have less than the minimum at another time, the time of industrial stagnation. That is to say, that during a certain space of time, which is always period-ical, in which trade passes through the circle of prosperity, overproduction, stagnation, crisis – that, taking the average of what the labourer received more, and what he received less, than the mini-mum, we shall find that on the whole he will have received neither more or less than the minimum; or, in other words, that the working class, as a class, will have conserved itself, after many miseries, many sufferings, and many corpses left upon the industrial battle field. But what matters that? The class exists, and not only it exists, but it will have increased. This law, that the lowest level of wages is the natural price of the commodity of labour, will realise itself in the same measure with Ricardo's supposition that Free Trade will become a reality. We accept every thing that has been said of the advantages of Free Trade. The powers of production will increase, the tax imposed upon the country by protective duties will disappear, all commodi-ties will be sold at a cheaper price. And what, again, says Ricardo? 'That labour being equally a commodity, will equally sell at a cheaper price' – that you will have it for very little money indeed, just as you will have pepper and salt. And then, in the same way as all other laws of political economy will receive an increased force, a surplus of truth, by the realisation of Free Trade – in the same way the law of population, as exposed by Malthus, will under the reign of Free Trade develop itself in as fine dimensions as can possibly be desired. Thus you have to choose: either you must disavow the whole of political economy as it exists at present, or you must allow that under the freedom of trade the whole severity of the laws of political economy will be applied to the working classes. Is that to say that we are against Free Trade? No, we are for Free Trade, because by Free Trade all economical laws, with their most astound-ing contradictions, will act upon a larger scale, upon a greater extent of territory, upon the territory of the whole earth; and because from the uniting of all these contradictions into a single group, where they stand face to face, will result the struggle which will itself eventuate in the emancipation of the proletarians.

Written at the end of September 1847
First published in *The Northern Star* No. 520, October 9, 1847 with an editorial note: 'From Our German Correspondent'
Reprinted from the newspaper

4

GENESIS OF THE INDUSTRIAL CAPITALIST

The genesis of the industrial[1] capitalist did not proceed in such a gradual way as that of the farmer. Doubtless many small guild-masters, and yet more independent small artisans, or even wage-labourers, transformed themselves into small capitalists, and (by gradually extending exploitation of wage-labour and corresponding accumulation) into full-blown capitalists. In the infancy of capitalist production, things often happened as in the infancy of mediaeval towns, where the question, which of the escaped serfs should be master and which servant, was in great part decided by the earlier or later date of their flight. The snail's pace of this method corresponded in no wise with the commercial requirements of the new world-market that the great discoveries of the end of the fifteenth century created. But the middle ages had handed down two distinct forms of capital, which mature in the most different economic social formations, and which, before the era of the capitalist mode of production, are considered as capital quand même – usurer's capital and merchant's capital.

'At present, all the wealth of society goes first into the possession of the capitalist ... he pays the landowner his rent, the labourer his wages, the tax and tithe gatherer their claims, and keeps a large, indeed the largest, and a continually augmenting share, of the annual produce of labour for himself. The capitalist may now be said to be the first owner of all the wealth of the community, though no law has conferred on him the right to this property ... this change has been effected by the taking of interest on capital ... and it is not a little curious that all the law-givers of Europe endeavoured to prevent this by statutes, viz., statutes against usury ... The power of the capitalist over all the wealth of the country is a complete change in the right of property, and by what law, or series of laws, was it effected?'[2] The author should have remembered that revolutions are not made by laws.

The money capital formed by means of usury and commerce was prevented from turning into industrial capital, in the country by the feudal constitution, in the towns by the guild organisation.[3] These fetters vanished with the dissolution of feudal society, with the expropriation and partial eviction of the country population. The new manufactures were established at sea-ports, or at inland points beyond the control of the old municipalities and their guilds. Hence in England an embittered struggle of the corporate towns against these new industrial nurseries.

The discovery of gold and silver in America, the extirpation, enslavement and entombment in mines of the aboriginal population, the beginning of the conquest and looting of the East Indies, the turning of Africa into a warren for the commercial hunting of black-skins, signalised the rosy dawn of the era of capitalist production. These idyllic proceedings are the chief momenta of primitive accumulation. On their heels treads the commercial war of the European nations, with the globe for a theatre. It begins with the revolt of the Netherlands from Spain, assumes giant dimensions in England's Anti-Jacobin War, and is still going on in the opium wars against China, &c.

The different momenta of primitive accumulation distribute themselves now, more or less in chronological order, particularly over Spain, Portugal, Holland, France, and England. In England at the end of the seventeenth century, they arrive at a systematical combination, embracing the colonies, the national debt, the modern mode of taxation, and the protectionist system. These methods depend in part on brute force, e.g., the colonial system. But they all employ the power of the State, the concentrated and organised force of society, to hasten, hot-house fashion, the process of transformation of the feudal mode of production into the capitalist mode, and to shorten the transition. Force is the midwife of every old society pregnant with a new one. It is itself an economic power.

Of the Christian colonial system, W. Howitt, a man who makes a speciality of Christianity, says: 'The barbarities and desperate outrages of the so-called Christian race, throughout every region of the world, and upon every people they have been able to subdue, are not to be paralleled by those of any other race, however fierce, however untaught, and however reckless of mercy and of shame, in any age of the earth'.[4] The history of the colonial administration of Holland – and Holland was the head capitalistic nation of the seventeenth century – 'is one of the most extraordinary relations of treachery, bribery, massacre, and meanness'.[5] Nothing is more characteristic than their system of stealing men, to get slaves for Java. The men stealers were trained for this purpose. The thief, the interpreter, and the seller, were the chief agents in this trade, native princes the chief sellers. The young people stolen, were thrown into the secret dungeons of Celebes, until they were ready for sending to the slave-ships. An official report says: 'This one town of Macassar, e.g., is full of secret prisons, one more horrible than the other, crammed with unfortunates, victims of greed and tyranny fettered in chains, forcibly torn from their families'. To secure Malacca, the Dutch corrupted the Portuguese governor. He let them into the town in 1641. They hurried at once to his house and assassinated him, to 'abstain' from the payment of £21,875, the price of his treason. Wherever they set foot, devastation and depopulation followed. Banjuwangi, a province of Java, in 1750 numbered over 80,000 inhabitants, in 1811 only 18,000. Sweet commerce!

The English East India Company, as is well known, obtained, besides the political rule in India, the exclusive monopoly of the tea-trade, as well as of the Chinese trade in general, and of the transport of goods to and from Europe. But the coasting trade of India and between the islands, as well as the internal trade of India, were the monopoly of the higher employés of the company. The monopolies of salt, opium, betel and other commodities, were inexhaustible mines of wealth. The employés themselves fixed the price and plundered at will the unhappy Hindus. The Governor-General took part in this private traffic. His favourites received contracts under conditions whereby they, cleverer than the alchemists, made gold out of nothing. Great fortunes sprang up like mushrooms in a day; primitive accumulation went on without the advance of a shilling. The trial of Warren Hastings swarms with such cases. Here is an instance. A contract for opium was given to a certain Sullivan at the moment of his departure on an official mission to a part of India far removed from the opium district. Sullivan sold his contract to one Binn for £40,000; Binn sold it the same day for £60,000, and the ultimate purchaser who carried out the contract declared that after all he realised an enormous gain. According to one of the lists laid before Parliament, the Company and its employés from 1757-1766 got £6,000,000 from the Indians as gifts. Between 1769 and 1770, the English manufactured a famine by buying up all the rice and refusing to sell it again, except at fabulous prices.[6]

The treatment of the aborigines was, naturally, most frightful, in plantation-colonies destined for export trade only, such as the West Indies, and in rich and well-populated countries, such as Mexico and India, that were given over to plunder. But even in the colonies properly so called, the Christian character of primitive accumulation did not belie itself. Those sober virtuosi of Protestantism, the Puritans of New England, in 1703, by decrees of their assembly set a premium of £40 on every Indian scalp and every captured red-skin: in 1720 a premium of £100 on every scalp; in 1744, after Massachusetts-Bay had proclaimed a certain tribe as rebels, the following prices: for a male scalp of 12 years and upwards £100 (new currency), for a male prisoner £105, for women and children prisoners, £50, for scalps of women and children £50. Some decades later, the colonial system took its revenge on the descendants of the pious pilgrim fathers, who had grown seditious in the meantime. At English instigation and for English pay they were tomahawked by red-skins. The British Parliament proclaimed blood-hounds and scalping as 'means that God and Nature had given into its hand'.

The colonial system ripened, like a hot-house, trade and navigation. The 'societies Monopolia' of Luther were powerful levers for concentration of capital. The colonies secured a market for the budding manufactures, and, through the monopoly of the market, an increased accumulation. The treasures captured outside Europe by undisguised looting, enslavement, and murder, floated back to the mother-country and were there turned into capital. Holland, which first fully developed the colonial system, in 1648 stood already in the acme of its commercial greatness. It was 'in almost exclusive possession of the East Indian trade and the commerce between the south-east and north-west of Europe. Its fisheries, marine, manufactures, surpassed those of any other country. The total capital of the Republic was probably more important than that of all the rest of Europe put together'. Gülich forgets to add that by 1648, the people of Holland were more overworked, poorer and more brutally oppressed than those of all the rest of Europe put together.

Today industrial supremacy implies commercial supremacy. In the period of manufacture properly so called, it is, on the other hand, the commercial supremacy that gives industrial predominance. Hence the preponderant rôle that the colonial system plays at that time. It was 'the strange God' who perched himself on the altar cheek by jowl with the old Gods of Europe, and one fine day with a shove and a kick chucked them all of a heap. It proclaimed surplus-value making as the sole end and aim of humanity.

The system of public credit, i.e., of national debts, whose origin we discover in Genoa and Venice as early as the middle ages, took possession of Europe generally during the manufacturing period. The colonial system with its maritime trade and commercial wars served as a forcing-house for it. Thus it first took root in Holland. National debts, i.e., the alienation of the state – whether despotic, constitutional or republican – marked with its stamp the capitalistic era. The only part of the so-called national wealth that actually enters into the collective possessions of modern people is – their national debt.[7] Hence, as a necessary consequence, the modern doctrine that a nation becomes the richer the more deeply it is in debt. Public credit becomes the *credo* of capital. And with the rise of national debt-making, want of faith in the national debt takes the place of the blasphemy against the Holy Ghost, which may not be forgiven.

The public debt becomes one of the most powerful levers of primitive accumulation. As with the stroke of an enchanter's wand, it endows barren money with the power of breeding and thus turns it into capital, without the necessity of its exposing itself to the troubles and risks inseparable from its employment in industry or even in usury. The state-creditors actually give nothing away, for the sum lent is transformed into public bonds, easily negotiable, which go on functioning in their hands just as so much hard cash would. But further, apart from the class of lazy annuitants thus created, and from the improvised wealth of the financiers, middlemen between the government and the nation – as also apart from the tax-farmers, merchants, private manufacturers, to whom a good part of every national loan renders the service of a capital fallen from heaven – the national debt has given rise to joint-stock companies, to dealings in negotiable effects of all kinds, and to agiotage, in a word to stock-exchange gambling and the modern bankocracy.

At their birth the great banks, decorated with national titles, were only associations of private speculators, who placed themselves by the side of governments, and, thanks to the privileges they received, were in a position to advance money to the State. Hence the accumulation of the national debt has no more infallible measure than the successive rise in the stock of these banks, whose full development dates from the founding of the Bank of England in 1694. The Bank of England began with lending its money to the Government at 8 per cent; at the same time it was empowered by Parliament to coin money out of the same capital, by lending it again to the public in the form of banknotes. It was allowed to use these notes for discounting bills, making advances on commodities, and for buying the precious metals. It was not long ere this credit-money, made by the bank itself, became the coin in which the Bank of England made its loans to the State, and paid, on account of the State, the interest on the public debt. It was not enough that the bank gave with one hand and took back more with the other; it remained, even whilst receiving, the eternal creditor of the nation down to the last shilling advanced. Gradually it became inevitably the receptacle of the metallic hoard of the country, and the centre of gravity of all commercial credit. What effect was produced on their contemporaries by the sudden uprising of this brood of bankocrats, financiers, rentiers, brokers, stock-jobbers, &c., is proved by the writings of that time, e.g., by Bolingbroke's.[8]

With the national debt arose an international credit system, which often conceals one of the sources of primitive accumulation in this or that people. Thus the villainies of the Venetian thieving system formed one of the secret bases of the capital-wealth of Holland to whom Venice in her decadence lent large sums of money. So also was it with Holland and England. By the beginning of the eighteenth century the Dutch manufactures were far outstripped. Holland had ceased to be the nation preponderant in commerce and industry. One of its main lines of business, therefore, from 1701-1776, is the lending out of enormous amounts of capital, especially to its great rival England. The same thing is going on to-day between England and the United States. A great deal of capital which appears to-day in the United States without any certificate of birth, was yesterday, in England, the capitalised blood of children.

As the national debt finds its support in the public revenue, which must cover the yearly payments for interest, &c., the modern system of taxation was the necessary complement of the system of national loans. The loans enable the government to meet extraordinary expenses, without the tax-payers feeling it immediately, but they necessitate, as a consequence, increased taxes. On the other hand, the raising of taxation caused by the accumulation of debts contracted one after another, compels the government always to have recourse to new loans for new extraordinary expenses. Modern fiscality, whose pivot is formed by taxes on the most necessary means of subsistence (thereby increasing their price), thus contains within itself the germ of automatic progression. Over-taxation is not an incident, but rather a principle. In Holland, therefore, where this system was first inaugurated, the great patriot, De Witt, has in his 'Maxims' extolled it as the best system for making the wage-labourer submissive, frugal, industrious, and overburdened with labour. The destructive influence that it exercises on the condition of the wage-labourer concerns us less however, here, than the forcible expropriation, resulting from it, of peasants, artisans, and in a word, all elements of the lower middle-class. On this there are not two opinions, even among the bourgeois economists. Its expropriating efficacy is still further heightened by the system of protection, which forms one of its integral parts.

The great part that the public debt, and the fiscal system corresponding with it, has played in the capitalisation of wealth and the expropriation of the masses, has led many writers, like Cobbett, Doubleday and others, to seek in this, incorrectly, the fundamental cause of the misery of the modern peoples.

The system of protection was an artificial means of manufacturing manufacturers, of expropriating independent labourers, of capitalising the national means of production and subsistence, of forcibly abbreviating the transition from the mediaeval to the modern mode of production. The European states tore one another to pieces about the patent of this invention, and, once entered into the service of the surplus-value makers, did not merely lay under contribution in the pursuit of this purpose their own people, indirectly through protective duties, directly through export premiums. They also forcibly rooted out, in their dependent countries, all industry, as, e.g., England did with the Irish woollen manufacture. On the continent of Europe, after Colbert's example, the process was much simplified. The primitive industrial capital, here, came in part directly out of the state treasury. 'Why,' cried Mirabeau, 'why go so far to seek the cause of the manufacturing glory of Saxony before the war? 180,000,000 of debts contracted by the sovereigns!'[9]

Colonial system, public debts, heavy taxes, protection, commercial wars, &c., these children of the true manufacturing period, increase gigantically during the infancy of Modern Industry. The birth of the latter is heralded by a great slaughter of the innocents. Like the royal navy, the factories were recruited by means of the press-gang. Blasé as Sir F.M. Eden is as to the horrors of the expropriation of the agricultural population from the soil, from the last third of the fifteenth century to his own time; with all the self-satisfaction with which he rejoices in this process, 'essential' for establishing capitalistic agriculture and 'the due proportion between arable and pasture land' – he does not show, however, the same economic insight in respect to the necessity of child-stealing and child-slavery for the transformation of manufacturing exploitation into factory exploitation, and the establishment of the 'true relation' between capital and labour-power. He says:

'It may, perhaps, be worthy the attention of the public to consider, whether any manufacture, which, in order to be carried on successfully, requires that cottages and workhouses should be ransacked for poor children; that they should be employed by turns during the greater part of the night and robbed of the rest which, though indispensable to all, is most required by the young; and that numbers of both sexes, of different ages and dispositions, should be collected together in such a manner that the contagion of example cannot but lead to profligacy and debauchery; will add to the sum of individual or national felicity?'[10]

'In the counties of Derbyshire, Nottinghamshire, and more particularly in Lancashire', says Fielden, 'the newly-invented machinery was used in large factories built on the sides of streams capable of turning the water-wheel. Thousands of hands were suddenly required in these places, remote from towns; and Lancashire, in particular, being, till then, comparatively thinly populated and barren, a population was all that she now wanted. The small and nimble fingers of little children being by very far the most in request, the custom instantly sprang up of procuring *apprentices* from the different parish workhouses of London, Birmingham, and elsewhere. Many, many thousands of these little, hapless creatures were sent down into the north, being from the age of 7 to the age of 13 or 14 years old. The custom was for the master to clothe his apprentices and to feed and lodge them in an 'apprentice house' near the factory; overseers were appointed to see to the works, whose interest it was to work the children to the utmost, because their pay was in proportion to the quantity of work that they could exact. Cruelty was, of course, the consequence ... In many of the manufacturing districts, but particularly, I am afraid, in the guilty country to which I belong [Lancashire], cruelties the most heart-rending were practised upon the unoffending and friendless creatures who were thus consigned to the charge of master-manufacturers; they were harassed to the brink of death by excess of labour ... were flogged, fettered and tortured in the most exquisite refinement of cruelty ... they were in many cases starved to the bone while flogged to their work and ... even in some instances ... were driven to commit suicide ... The beautiful and romantic valleys of Derbyshire, Nottinghamshire and Lancashire, secluded from the public eye, became the dismal solitudes of torture, and of many a murder. The profits of manufacturers were enormous; but this only whetted the appetite that it should have satisfied, and therefore the manufacturers had recourse to an expedient that seemed to secure to them those profits without any possibility of limit; they began the practice of what is termed 'night-working', that is, having tired one set of hands, by working them throughout the day, they had another set ready to go on working throughout the night; the day-set getting into the beds that the night-set had just quitted, and in their turn again, the night-set getting into the beds that the day-set quitted in the morning. It is a common tradition in Lancashire, that the beds *never get cold*'.[11]

With the development of capitalist production during the manufacturing period, the public opinion of Europe had lost the last remnant of shame and conscience. The nations bragged cynically of every infamy that served them as a means to capitalistic accumulation. Read, e.g., the naïve Annals of Commerce of the worthy A. Anderson. Here it is trumpeted forth as a triumph of English statecraft that at the Peace of Utrecht, England extorted from the Spaniards by the Asiento Treaty the privilege of being allowed to ply the negro-trade, until then only carried on between Africa and the English West Indies, between Africa and Spanish America as well. England thereby acquired the right of supplying Spanish America until 1743 with 4,800 negroes yearly. This threw, at the same time, an official cloak over British smuggling. Liverpool waxed fat on the slave-trade. This was its method of primitive accumulation. And, even to the present day, Liverpool 'respectability' is the Pindar of the slave-trade which – compare the work of Aikin [1795] already quoted – 'has coincided with that spirit of bold adventure which has characterised the trade of Liverpool and rapidly carried it to its present state of prosperity; has occasioned vast employment for shipping and sailors, and greatly augmented the demand for the manufactures of the country' (p339). Liverpool employed in the slave-trade, in 1730, 15 ships; in 1751, 53; in 1760, 74; in 1770, 96; and in 1792, 132.

Whilst the cotton industry introduced child-slavery in England, it gave in the United States a stimulus to the transformation of the earlier, more or less patriarchal slavery, into a system of commercial exploitation. In fact, the veiled slavery of the wage-workers in Europe needed, for its pedestal, slavery pure and simple in the new world.[12]

Tantæ molis erat, to establish the 'eternal laws of Nature' of the capitalist mode of production, to complete the process of separation between labourers and conditions of labour, to transform, at one pole, the social means of production and subsistence into capital, at the opposite pole, the mass of the population into wage-labourers, into 'free labouring poor', that artificial product of modern society.[13] If money, according to Augier, 'comes into the world with a congenital blood-stain on one cheek',[14] capital comes dripping from head to foot, from every pore, with blood and dirt.[15]

NOTES

1. Industrial here in contradistinction to agricultural. In the 'categoric' sense the farmer is an industrial capitalist as much as the manufacturer.

2. 'The Natural and Artificial Rights of Property Contrasted' London, 1832, pp98-99. Author of the anonymous work: 'Th. Hodgskin.'

3. Even as late as 1794, the small cloth-makers of Leeds sent a deputation to Parliament, with a petition for a law to forbid any merchant from becoming a manufacturer. (Dr J. Aikin, *A Description of the Country from Thirty to Forty Miles round Manchester*, London 1795).

4. William Howitt: *Colonisation and Christianity: A Popular History of the Treatment of the Natives by the Europeans in all their Colonies*, London 1838, p9. On the treatment of the slaves there is a good compilation in Charles Conte, *Traité de la Législation*, (3me éd), Bruxelles 1837. This subject one must study in detail, to see what the bourgeoisie makes of itself and of the labourer, wherever it can, without restraint, model the world after its own image.

5. Thomas Stamford Raffles, late Lieut-Gov. of that island: *The History of Java and its dependencies*, London 1817.

6. In the year 1866 more than a million Hindus died of hunger in the province of Orissa alone. Nevertheless, the attempt was made to enrich the Indian treasury by the price at which the necessaries of life were sold to the starving people.

7. William Cobbett remarks that in England all public institutions are designated 'royal'; as compensation for this, however, there is the 'national' debt.

8. 'Si les Tartares inondaient l'Europe aujourd'hui, il faudrait bien des

affaires pour leur faire entendre ce que c'est qu'un financier parmi noud',
Montesquieu, *Oeuvres. De l'esprit des lois*, t. iv., p33, ed. Londres 1769.

9. H.G.R. Mirabeau, *De la monarchie prussienne sous Frédéric le Grand*,
   Londres 1788, t. vi., p101.

10. F.M. Eden, *The State of the Poor: or, an history of the labouring classes in
    England, from the conquest to the present period*, London 1797, vol. I.,
    book II, ch. 1., p421.

11. John Fielden, *The Curse of the Factory System: or, a short account of the
    origin of factory cruelties*, London 1836, pp5, 6. On the earlier infamies of
    the factory system see Dr J. Aikin, *A Description of the Country from
    Thirty to Forty miles round Manchester*, London 1795, p219; and
    Gisborne, *An Enquiry into the Duties of Men in the Higher and Middle
    Classes of Society in Great Britain, Resulting from Their Respective
    Stations, Professions, and Employments*, London 1795, vol. II. When the
    steam-engine transplanted the factories from the country waterfalls to the
    middle of towns, the 'abstemious' surplus-value maker found the child-
    material ready to his hand, without being forced to seek slaves from the
    workhouses. When Sir R. Peel (father of the 'minister of plausibility'),
    brought in his bill for the protection of children, in 1815, Francis Horner,
    lumen of the Billion Committee and intimate friend of Ricardo, said in the
    House of Commons: 'It is notorious, that with a bankrupt's effects, a gang,
    if he might use the word, of these children had been put up to sale, and
    were advertised publicly as part of the property. A most atrocious instance
    had been brought before the Court of King's Bench two years before, in
    which a number of these boys, apprenticed by a parish in London to one
    manufacturer, had been transferred to another, and had been found by
    some benevolent persons in a state of absolute famine. Another case more
    horrible had come to his knowledge while on a [Parliamentary]
    Committee ... that not many years ago, an agreement had been made
    between a London parish and a Lancashire manufacturer, by which it was
    stipulated, that with every 20 sound children one idiot should be taken'.

12. In 1790, there were in the English West Indies ten slaves for one free man,
    in the French fourteen for one, in the Dutch twenty-three for one. Henry
    Brougham, *An Inquiry into the Colonial Policy of the European Powers*,
    Edinburgh 1803, vol. II, p74.

13. The phrase, 'labouring poor', is found in English legislation from the
    moment when the class of wage-labourers becomes noticeable. This terms
    is used in opposition, on the one hand, to the 'idle poor', beggars, etc., on
    the other to those labourers, who, pigeons not yet plucked, are still posses-
    sors of their own means of labour. From the Statute Book it passed into
    Political Economy, and was handed down by Culpeper, J. Child, etc., to

Adam Smith and Eden. After this, one can judge of the good faith of the 'execrable political cant-monger', Edmund Burke, when he called the expression, 'labouring poor', – 'execrable political cant'. This sycophant who, in the pay of the English oligarchy, played the romantic laudator temporis acti against the French Revolution, just as, in the pay of the North American Colonies, at the beginning of the American troubles, he had played the Liberal against the English oligarchy, was an out and out vulgar bourgeois. 'The laws of commerce are the laws of Nature, and therefore the laws of God', E. Burke, *Thoughts and Details on Scarcity*, London 1800, pp31, 32. No wonder that, true to the laws of God and of Nature he always sold himself in the best market. A very good portrait of this Edmund Burke, during his liberal time, is to be found in the writings of the Rev. Mr. Tucker. Tucker was a parson and a Tory, but, for the rest, an honourable man and a competent political economist. In face of the infamous cowardice of character that reigns today, and believes most devoutly in 'the laws of commerce', it is our bounden duty again and again to brand the Burkes, who only differ from their successors in one thing – talent.

14. Marie Augier, *Du Crédit Public*, Paris 1842.

15. 'Capital is said by a Quarterly Reviewer to fly turbulence and strife, and to be timid, which is very true; but this is very incompletely stating the question. Capital eschews no profit, or very small profit, just as Nature was formerly said to abhor a vacuum. With adequate profit, capital is very bold. A certain 10 per cent will ensure its employment anywhere; 20 per cent, certain will produce eagerness; 50 per cent, positive audacity; 100 per cent will make it ready to trample on all human laws; 300 per cent, and there is not a crime at which it will scruple, nor a risk it will not run, even to the chance of its owner being hanged. If turbulence and strife will bring a profit, it will freely encourage both. Smuggling and the slave-trade have amply proved all that is here stated', T.J. Dunning, *Trades' Unions and Strikes: Their Philosophy and Intention*, London 1860, pp35, 36.

5

ENGLAND IN 1845 AND 1885

For England, the effects of this domination of the manufacturing capitalists were at first startling. Trade revived and extended to a degree unheard of even in this cradle of modern industry; the previous astounding creations of steam and machinery dwindled into nothing compared with the immense mass of productions of the twenty years from 1850 to 1870, with the overwhelming figures of exports and imports, of wealth accumulated in the hands of capitalists and of human working power concentrated in the large towns. The progress was indeed interrupted, as before, by a crisis every ten years, in 1857 as well as in 1866; but these revulsions were now considered as natural, inevitable events, which must be fatalistically submitted to, and which always set themselves right in the end.

And the condition of the working class during this period? There was temporary improvement even for the great mass. But this improvement always was reduced to the old level by the influx of the great body of the unemployed reserve, by the constant superseding of hands by new machinery, by the immigration of the agricultural population, now, too, more and more superseded by machines.

A permanent improvement can be recognised for two 'protected' sections only of the working class. Firstly, the factory hands. The fixing by Act of Parliament of their working day within relatively rational limits, has restored their physical constitution and endowed them with a moral superiority, enhanced by their local concentration. They are undoubtedly better off than before 1848. The best proof is that out of ten strikes they make, nine are provoked by the manufacturers in their own interests, as the only means of securing a reduced production. You can never get the masters to agree to work 'short time', let manufactured goods be ever so unsaleable; but get the workpeople to strike, and the masters shut their factories to a man.

Secondly, the great Trades' Unions. They are the organisations of those trades in which the labour of *grown-up* men predominates, or is alone applicable. Here the competition neither of women and children nor of machinery has so far weakened their organised strength. The engineers, the carpenters and joiners, the bricklayers, are each of them a power, to that extent that, as in the case of the bricklayers and bricklayers' labourers, they can even successfully resist the introduction of machinery. That their condition has remarkably improved since 1848 there can be no doubt and the best proof of this is in the fact that for more than fifteen years not only have their employers been with them, but they with their employers, upon exceedingly good terms. They form an aristocracy among the working class; they have succeeded in enforcing for themselves a relatively comfortable position, and they accept it as final. They are the model working men of Messrs Leone Levi and Giffen, and they are very nice people indeed nowadays to deal with, for any sensible capitalist in particular and for the whole capitalist class in general.

But as to the great mass of the working people, the state of misery and insecurity in which they live now is as low as ever, if not lower. The East-end of London is an ever-spreading pool of stagnant misery and desolation, of starvation when out of work, and degradation, physical and moral, when in work. And so in all other large towns – abstraction made of the privileged minority of the workers; and so in the smaller towns and in the agricultural districts. The law which reduces the *value* of labor-power to the value of the necessary means of subsistence, and the other law which reduces its *average price* as a rule to the minimum of those means of subsistence: these laws act upon them with the irresistible force of an automatic engine, which crushes them between its wheels.

This, then, was the position created by the Free Trade policy of 1847, and by twenty years of the rule of the manufacturing capitalists. But then a change came. The crash of 1866 was, indeed, followed by a slight and short revival about 1873; but that did not last. We did not, indeed, pass through the full crisis at the time it was due, in 1877 or 1878; but we have had, ever since 1876, a chronic state of stagnation in all dominant branches of industry. Neither will the full crash come; nor will the period of longed-for prosperity to which we used to be entitled before and after it. A dull depression, a chronic glut of all markets for all trades, that is what we have been living in for nearly ten years. How is this?

The Free Trade theory was based upon one assumption: that England was to be the one great manufacturing centre of an agricultural world. And the actual fact is that this assumption has turned out to be a pure delusion. The conditions of modern industry, steam-power and machinery, can be established wherever there is fuel, especially coals. And other countries beside England: France, Belgium, Germany, America, even Russia, have coals. And the people over there did not see the advantage of being turned into Irish pauper farmers merely for the greater wealth and glory of English capitalists. They set resolutely about manufacturing, not only for themselves but for the rest of the world; and the consequence is, that the manufacturing monopoly enjoyed by England for nearly a century is irretrievably broken up.

But the manufacturing monopoly of England is the pivot of the present social system of England. Even while that monopoly lasted the markets could not keep pace with the increasing productivity of English manufacturers; the decennial crises were the consequence. And now markets are getting scarcer every day, so much so that even the negroes of the Congo are now to be forced into the civilisation attendant upon Manchester calicoes, Staffordshire pottery, and Birmingham hardware. How will it be when Continental, and especially American goods, flow in ever increasing quantities – when the predominating share, still held by British manufacturers, will become reduced from year to year? Answer, Free Trade, thou universal panacea?

I am not the first to point this out. Already, in 1883, at the Southport meeting of the British Association, Mr Inglis Palgrave, the President of the Economical section, stated plainly that:

the days of great trade profits in England were over, and there was a pause in the progress of several great branches of industrial labour. The country might almost be said to be entering the non-progressive state.[1]

But what is to be the consequence? Capitalist production *cannot* stop. It must go on increasing and expanding, or it must die. Even now, the mere reduction of England's lion's share in the supply of the world's markets means stagnation, distress, excess of capital here, excess of unemployed work-people there. What will it be when the increase of yearly production is brought to a complete stop?

Here is the vulnerable place, the heel of Achilles, for capitalist production. Its very basis is the necessity of constant expansion, and this constant expansion now becomes impossible. It ends in a deadlock. Every year England is brought nearer face to face with the question: either the country must go to pieces, or capitalist production must. Which is it to be?

And the working class? If even under the unparalleled commercial and industrial expansion, from 1848 to 1868, they have had to undergo such misery; if even then the great bulk of them experienced at best a temporary improvement of their condition, while only a small, privileged, 'protected' minority was permanently benefited, what will it be when this dazzling period is brought finally to a close; when the present dreary stagnation shall not only become intensified, but this its intensified condition shall become the permanent and normal state of English trade?

The truth is this: during the period of England's industrial monopoly the English working class have to a certain extent shared in the benefits of the monopoly. These benefits were very unequally parcelled out amongst them; the privileged minority pocketed most, but even the great mass had at least a temporary share now and then. And that is the reason why since the dying-out of Owenism there has been no Socialism in England. With the breakdown of that monopoly the English working class will lose that privileged position; it will find itself generally – the privileged and leading minority not excepted – on a level with its fellow-workers abroad. And that is the reason why there will be Socialism again in England.

Frederick Engels

Written in mid-February 1885
First published in *The Commonweal*, No. 2, March 1885.
Reproduced from the magazine collated with the German translation

NOTE
1. Address by R.H. Inglis Palgrave, F.R.S., F.S.S., President of the Section in Report of the *Fifty-Third Meeting of the British Association for the Advancement of Science* held at Southport in September 1883, pp608-09. [*Ed*]

Section 3: The Inevitability of Development?

6. Karl Marx, 'Letter to *Otechestvenniye Zapiski*' (1877), *Marx and Engels Collected Works*, vol. 24, pp196-201.

7. Karl Marx, 'Third draft of letter to Vera Zasulich' (1881), *Marx and Engels Collected Works*, vol. 24, pp364-369.

Globalisation theory takes the newest features of the economy – the spread of computers, the internationalisation of trade and production – and argues that these new aspects will re-shape the economy as a whole. In some ways Marx's method was similar, when Marx and Engels wrote about capitalism they took their examples from Britain, and assumed that the whole world would follow that lead. But in the 1840s, Britain was exceptional. Only three or four other countries were already urban and industrialised. So the argument that one sector of the economy is now the most dynamic – does not mean that this sector will necessarily come to dominate the rest. Fashions change. At the start of the 1990s, every management consultant praised 'Japanisation', but ten years of slump in the Japanese economy suggests to people today that this was not such an ideal path to follow.

This section examines Marx's belief that more than one route to industrialisation was possible. Karl Marx wrote these letters in response to specific enquiries from prominent Russian socialists. Although probably not intended for publication, these comments were certainly written to generate wide discussion. The letters were unusually provisional and uncertain in tone. With the letter to Vera Zasulich, Marx penned three long drafts (the third is included here), before settling on a much shorter final note.

Karl Marx was rarely so equivocal – why was he so cautious now? The matter under discussion was the future of Russia, then one of the great military powers of Europe, yet otherwise an underdeveloped, backward country on the periphery of capitalist development. Marx did not believe that Russia had to follow the 'English' model, forcing the peasants off the land, as the preliminary step towards creating modern industry. Yet Marx was also wary of the counter-argument that Russia might find its own peasant path to socialism, by-passing capitalism along the way. Marx clearly hoped that more than one route was available to achieve industrialisation, or indeed socialism. But Karl Marx ran shy of forecasting how such paths would be achieved. Rather than predicting the future, Marx and Engels preferred to look to the present, to find the openings which were most pregnant with the hope for change.

6

KARL MARX
[LETTER TO OTECHESTVENNIYE ZAPISKI]

Dear Sir,[1]

The author[2] of the article 'Karl Marx Before the Tribunal of Mr Zhukovsky' is obviously an intelligent man and, had he found a single passage in my account of 'primitive accumulation' to support his conclusions, he would have quoted it. For want of such a passage he considers it necessary to seize hold of an annexe, a polemical sortie against a Russian 'belletrist'[3] printed in the appendix to the first German edition of *Capital*. What do I there reproach this writer for? The fact that he discovered 'Russian' communism not in Russia but in the book of Haxthausen,[4] the adviser to the Prussian Government, and that in his hands the Russian community serves only as an argument to prove that the old, rotten Europe must be regenerated by the victory of Pan-Slavism. My appreciation of this writer may be correct, it may be wrong, but in neither case could it provide the key to my views on the efforts 'of Russians to find a path of development for their country which will be different from that which Western Europe pursued and still pursues etc.'[5]

In the Afterword to the second German edition of *Capital* – which the author of the article about Mr Zhukovsky knows, because he quoted it – I speak of 'a great Russian scholar and critic' with the high esteem which he deserves.[6] In his noteworthy articles the latter dealt with the question whether Russia should start, as its liberal economists wish, by destroying the rural community in order to pass to a capitalist system or whether, on the contrary, it can acquire all the fruits of this system without suffering its torments, by developing its own historical conditions. He comes out in favour of the second solution. And my honourable critic would have been at least as justified in inferring from my esteem for this 'great Russian scholar and critic' that I shared his views on this question as he is in concluding from my polemic against the 'belletrist' and Pan-Slavist that I rejected them.

Be that as it may, as I do not like to leave anything to 'guesswork', I shall speak straight out. In order to reach an informed judgement of the economic development of contemporary Russia, I learned Russian and then spent several long years studying official publications and others with a bearing on this subject. I have arrived at this result: if Russia continues along the path it has followed since 1861, it will miss the finest chance that history has ever offered to a nation, only to undergo all the fatal vicissitudes of the capitalist system.

The chapter on primitive accumulation does not pretend to do more than trace the road by which in Western Europe the capitalist economic order emerged from the entrails of the feudal economic order. It thus describes the historical movement which by divorcing the producers from their means of production transforms them into wage-workers (proletarians in the modern sense of the word) and the owners of the means of production into capitalists. In this history, 'every revolution which acts as a lever for the advancement of the capitalist class in its process of formation marks an epoch; above all that which, by stripping great masses of men of their traditional means of production and subsistence, suddenly hurls them on the labour market. But the basis of this whole development is the expropriation of the agricultural producer. To date this has not been accomplished in a radical fashion anywhere except in England ... but all the other countries of Western Europe are undergoing the same process etc.' (*Capital*, French edition, p315). At the end of the chapter the historical tendency of capitalist production is summed up thus: That it 'itself begets its own negation with the inexorability which governs the metamorphoses of nature'; that it has itself created the elements of a new economic order, by giving the greatest impulse at once to the productive forces of social labour and to the integral development of every individual producer; that capitalist property, which actually rests already on a collective mode of production, can only be transformed into social property.

I do not give any proof at this point for the very good reason that this assertion itself is nothing but a summary recapitulation of long developments previously set out in the chapters on capitalist production.

Now, in what way was my critic able to apply this historical sketch to Russia?[7] Only this: if Russia is tending to become a capitalist nation, on the model of the countries of Western Europe – and in recent years it has gone to great pains to move in this direction – it will not succeed without having first transformed a large proportion of its peasants into proletarians; and after that, once it has been placed in the bosom of the capitalist system, it will be subjected to its pitiless laws, like other profane peoples. That is all! But this is too little for my critic. It is absolutely necessary for him to metamorphose my historical sketch of the genesis of capitalism in Western Europe into a historico-philosophical theory of general development, imposed by fate on all peoples, whatever the historical circumstances in which they are placed, in order to eventually attain this economic formation which, with a tremendous leap of the productive forces of social labour, assures the most integral development of every individual producer. But I beg his pardon. This does me too much honour, and yet puts me to shame at the same time. Let us take an example. In various places in *Capital* I allude to the destiny of the plebeians of Ancient Rome. They were originally free peasants cultivating their own plots of land on their own account. In the course of Roman history they were expropriated. The same movement which cut them off from their means of production and subsistence involved not only the formation of large landed property but also the formation of large money capital. Thus, one fine morning, there were on the one hand free men stripped of everything except their labour power, and on the other, in order to exploit this labour, the owners of all the acquired wealth. What happened? The Roman proletarians became not wage labourers but an idle 'MOB', more abject than the former 'POOR WHITES' of the southern states of America; and alongside them there developed a mode of production that was not capitalist but based on slavery. Thus events strikingly analogous, but occurring in different historical milieux, led to quite disparate results. By studying each of these evolutions on its own, and then comparing them, one will easily discover the key to the phenomenon, but it will never be arrived at by employing the all-purpose formula of a general historico-philosophical theory whose supreme virtue consists in being supra-historical.

Written presumably in November 1877
First published in *Vestnik Narodnoi Voli,* No. 5, Geneva, 1886
Printed according to the manuscript
Translated from the French

NOTES

1. M. Ye. Saltykov-Shchedrin. [*Ed.*]
2. N.K. Mikhailovsky. [*Ed.*]
3. A.I. Herzen. [*Ed.*]
4. A. von Haxthausen, *Studien über die innern Zustände, das Volksleben und insbesondere die ländlichen Einrichtungen Rußlands*, Hannover 1847, Berlin 1852. [*Ed.*]
5. In Russian in the original. [*Ed.*]
6. N.G. Chernyshevsky. [Ed.]
7. N.K. Mikhailovsky. [Ed.]

7

[THIRD DRAFT]

Dear Citizen,

To deal thoroughly with the questions posed in your letter of February 16 I would have to go into matters in detail and break off urgent work, but the concise exposé which I have the honour of presenting to you will, I trust, suffice to dispel any misunderstandings with regard to my so-called theory.

I. In analysing the genesis of capitalist production I say: 'At the core of the capitalist system, therefore, lies the complete separation of the producer from the means of production ... the basis of this whole development is *the expropriation of the agricultural producer*. To date this has not been accomplished in a radical fashion anywhere except in England ... *But all the other countries of Western Europe* are undergoing the same process' (*Capital*, French ed., p315).

Hence the 'historical inevitability' of this process is *expressly* limited to the *countries of Western Europe*. The cause of that limitation is indicated in the following passage from Chapter XXXII: '*Private property, based on personal labour*... will be supplanted by *capitalist private property*, based on the exploitation of the labour of others, on wage labour' (*Capital*, French ed., p341).

In this Western movement, therefore, what is taking place is the *transformation of one form of private property into another form of private property*. In the case of the Russian peasants, *their communal property* would, on the contrary, have to be *transformed into private property*. Whether one asserts or denies the inevitability of that transformation, the reasons for and against have nothing to do with my analysis of the genesis of the capitalist system. At the very most one might infer from it that, given the present state of the great majority of

73

Russian peasants, the act of converting them into small proprietors would merely be the prelude to their rapid expropriation.

II. The most serious argument which has been put forward against the Russian commune amounts to this:

Go back to the origins of Western societies and everywhere you will find communal ownership of the land; with social progress it has everywhere given way to private property; so it will not be able to escape the same fate in Russia alone.

I will not take this argument into account except in so far as it is based on European experiences. As for the East Indies, for example, everyone except Sir Henry Maine and others of his ilk realises that the suppression of communal landownership out there was nothing but an act of English vandalism, pushing the native people not forwards but backwards.

Primitive communities are not all cast from the same die. On the contrary, taken all together, they form a series of social groupings which differ in both type and age, marking successive stages of evolution. One of these types, which convention terms *the agricultural commune*, is also that of the *Russian commune*. Its counterpart in the West is the *Germanic commune*, which is of very recent date. It did not yet exist in the days of Julius Caesar, nor did it exist any longer when the Germanic tribes came to conquer Italy, Gaul, Spain, etc. In Julius Caesar's day there was already an annual share-out of the arable land between groups, the *gentes* and the *tribes*, but not yet between the individual families of a commune; farming was probably also carried out in groups, communally. On Germanic soil itself this community of the archaic type turned, by natural development, into the *agricultural commune* as described by Tacitus. From that time on we lose sight of it. It perished obscurely amidst incessant wars and migrations; perhaps it died a violent death. But its natural viability is proved by two incontestable facts. Some scattered examples of this model survived all the vicissitudes of the Middle Ages and have been preserved into our own day, for instance the district of Trier in my own country. But, more importantly, we find the imprint of this 'agricultural commune' so clearly traced on the commune that succeeded it that Maurer, in analysing the latter, was able to reconstruct the former. The new commune, in which arable land belongs to its cultivators as *private property*, at the same time as forests, pastures, common lands, etc., remain *communal property*, was introduced by the Germanic peoples in all the countries which they conquered. Thanks to the characteristics borrowed from its prototype, it became the sole centre of popular liberty and life throughout the Middle Ages.

The 'rural commune' is also found in Asia, among the Afghans, etc., but everywhere it appears as the *most recent type* and, so to speak, as the last word in the *archaic formation* of societies. It is in order to emphasise this fact that I went into the Germanic commune in some detail.

We must now consider the most characteristic features distinguishing the 'agricultural commune' from more archaic communities.

1) All other communities are based on blood relations between their members. One cannot enter them unless one is a natural or adopted relative. Their structure is that of a family tree. The 'agricultural commune' was the first social groupings of free men not held together by blood-ties.

2) In the agricultural commune, the house and its complement, the courtyard, belonged to the agricultural producer as an individual. The *communal house* and *collective dwelling*, on the other hand, were the economic basis of more primitive communities, long before the introduction of the pastoral or agrarian way of life. True, one finds agricultural communes where the houses, despite having ceased to be collective dwelling places, periodically change owners. Individual usufruct is thus combined with communal property. But such communes still carry their birthmark: they are in a state of transition between a more archaic community and the agricultural commune proper.

3) The arable land, inalienable and communal property, is periodically divided between members of the agricultural commune in such a way that everyone tills the fields assigned to him on his own account and appropriates the fruits thereof as an individual. In more primitive communities the work is carried out communally and the communal

product is shared out according as it is required for consumption, excepting the portion reserved for reproduction.

One can understand that the *dualism* inherent in the constitution of the agricultural commune is able to endow it with a vigorous life. Freed from the strong but tight bonds of natural kinship, communal ownership of the land and the social relations stemming from it guarantee it a solid foundation, at the same time as the house and the courtyard, the exclusive domain of the individual family, parcel farming and the private appropriation of its fruits give a scope to individuality incompatible with the organism of more primitive communities.

But it is no less evident that in time this very dualism might turn into the germ of decomposition. Apart from all the malign influences from without, the commune carries the elements of corruption in its own bosom. Private landed property has already slipped into it in the guise of a house with its rural courtyard, which can be turned into a stronghold from which to launch the assault on the communal land. That is nothing new. But the vital thing is parcel labour as a source of private appropriation. It gives way to the accumulation of personal chattels, for example cattle, money and sometimes even slaves or serfs. This movable property, beyond the control of the commune, subject to individual exchanges in which guile and accident have their chance, will weigh more and more heavily on the entire rural economy. There we have the destroyer of primitive economic and social equality. It introduces heterogeneous elements, provoking in the bosom of the commune conflicts of interests and passions designed first to encroach on the communal ownership of arable lands, and then that of the forests, pastures, common lands, etc., which once converted into *communal appendages* of private property will fall to it in the long run.

As the last phase of the primitive formation of society, the agricultural commune is, at the same time, a transitional stage leading to the secondary formation, and hence marks the transition from a society founded on communal property to a society founded on private property. The secondary formation, of course, includes the series of societies resting on slavery and serfdom.

But does this mean to say that the historical career of the agricultural commune must inevitably come to such an end? Not at all. Its innate dualism admits of an alternative: either the property element will gain the upper hand over the collective element, or vice versa. It all depends on the historical environment in which the commune is placed.

Let us discount for the time being all the miseries besetting the agricultural commune in Russia and consider only its capacity for further development. It occupies a unique position, without precedent in history. Alone in Europe, it is still the predominant organic form of rural life throughout an immense empire. The common ownership of land provides it with the natural basis for collective appropriation, and its historical setting, its contemporaneity with capitalist production, lends it – fully developed – the material conditions for cooperative labour organised on a vast scale. It can thus incorporate the positive acquisitions devised by the capitalist system without passing through its Caudine Forks. It can gradually replace parcel farming with combined agriculture assisted by machines, which the physical lie of the land in Russia invites. Having been first restored to a normal footing in its present form, it may become the *direct starting point* for the economic system towards which modern society tends and turn over a new leaf without beginning by committing suicide.

The English themselves attempted some such thing in the East Indies; all they managed to do was to ruin native agriculture and double the number and severity of the famines.

But what about the anathema which affects the commune – its isolation, the lack of connexion between the life of one commune and that of the others, this *localised microcosm* which has hitherto prevented it from taking any historical initiative? It would vanish amidst a general turmoil in Russian society.

The familiarity of the Russian peasant with the *artel* would especially facilitate the transition from parcel labour to cooperative labour, which he already applies anyway, to a certain extent, in the tedding of the meadows and such communal undertakings as the land drainage, etc. A quite archaic peculiarity, the pet aversion of modern agronomists, still tends in this direction. If on arriving in any country you find that the arable land shows traces of a strange dismemberment, lending it the appearance of a chessboard composed of small fields, you need be in no doubt that it is the domain of an extinct agricultural commune! Its members, without having studied the theory of ground rent, perceived that the same amount of labour, expended on fields differing in natural fertility and location, will give differing yields. To spread the fortunes of labour more evenly, they therefore divided the land first into a certain number of areas, determined by the natural and economic divergences of the soil, and then broke up all these larger areas into as many parcels as there were labourers. Then each man was given a plot of land in each area. It goes without saying that this arrangement, perpetuated by the Russian commune into our own day, is at odds with the requirements of agronomy. Apart from other disadvantages, it entails a waste of energy and time. Nevertheless, it favours the transition to collective farming, with which it seems to be so much at odds at first glance. The parcel ...[1]

Written in late February and early March 1881
First published in Marx-Engels Archives, Book 1, Moscow, 1925
Printed according to *Marx-Engels gesamtausgabe (MEGA)*, Erste Abteilung, Band 25, Berlin, 1985, collated with the manuscript
Translated from the French

NOTE
1. The manuscript breaks off here. [*Ed.*]

Section 4: Imperialism

8. Karl Marx, 'Revolution in China and in Europe' (1853), *Marx and Engels Collected Works*, vol. 12, pp93-100

9. Karl Marx, 'Future results of British Rule in India' (1853), *Marx and Engels Collected Works*, vol. 12, pp217-223

10. Karl Marx, 'The Indian Revolt' (1857), *Marx and Engels Collected Works*, vol. 15, pp353-356

One part of the globalisation debate is an argument about the future of the relationship between different regions. Some writers expect globalisation to reduce the gap between regions – others point out that the Third World's share of world production and trade is actually falling. One hundred and fifty years ago, as today, the relationship between regions was in flux. For many centuries, non-European societies including China and India were at the forefront of technological development. Yet by the 1850s they had become stagnant. These empires found themselves under attack by foreign colonial powers. This process culminated in the 'Scramble for Africa' of the 1880s and 1890s. The supporters of the market promised that free trade would make the world more equal and more free. In reality, this wave of capitalist development brought only suffering in its wake.

These three pieces of journalism were published in the *New York Daily Tribune*, then the world's best-selling newspaper. Karl Marx became its European correspondent in 1851, and continued to write for the paper (with some help from Frederick Engels) for the next twelve years. Several of his articles dealt with developments in the British colonies, others described events back home. These pieces describe revolts against colonial power. Almost alone among his contemporaries in Britain, Marx sided with the victims of Empire against its instigators. At each stage, he blamed the British for the violence which accompanied resistance against their rule.

8

KARL MARX
REVOLUTION IN CHINA AND IN EUROPE

A most profound yet fantastic speculator on the principles which govern the movements of Humanity, was wont to extol as one of the ruling secrets of nature, what he called the law of the contact of extremes.[1] The homely proverb that 'extremes meet' was, in his view, a grand and potent truth in every sphere of life; an axiom with which the philosopher could as little dispense as the astronomer with the laws of Kepler or the great discovery of Newton.

Whether the 'contact of extremes' be such a universal principle or not, a striking illustration of it may be seen in the effect the Chinese revolution seems likely to exercise upon the civilised world. It may seem a very strange, and a very paradoxical assertion that the next uprising of the people of Europe, and their next movement for republican freedom and economy of government, may depend more probably on what is now passing in the Celestial Empire – the very opposite of Europe – than on any other political cause that now exists – more even than on the menaces of Russia and the consequent likelihood of a general European war. But yet it is no paradox, as all may understand by attentively considering the circumstances of the case.

Whatever be the social causes, and whatever religious, dynastic, or national shape they may assume, that have brought about the chronic rebellions subsisting in China for about ten years past, and now gathered together in one formidable revolution, the occasion of this outbreak has unquestionably been afforded by the English cannon forcing upon China that soporific drug called opium. Before the British arms the authority of the Manchu dynasty fell to pieces; the superstitious faith in the eternity of the Celestial Empire broke down; the barbarous and hermetic isolation from the civilised world was infringed; and an opening was made for that intercourse which has since proceeded so rapidly under the golden attractions of California and Australia. At the same time the silver coin of the Empire, its lifeblood, began to be drained away to the British East Indies.

Up to 1830, the balance of trade being continually in favour of the Chinese, there existed an uninterrupted importation of silver from India, Britain and the United States into China. Since 1833, and especially since 1840, the export of silver from China to India has become almost exhausting for the Celestial Empire. Hence the strong decrees of the Emperor against the opium trade, responded to by still stronger resistance to his measures. Besides this immediate economical consequence, the bribery connected with opium smuggling has entirely demoralised the Chinese State officers in the Southern provinces. Just as the Emperor was wont to be considered the father of all China, so his officers were looked upon as sustaining the paternal relation to their respective districts. But this patriarchal authority, the only moral link embracing the vast machinery of the State, has gradually been corroded by the corruption of those officers, who have made great gains by conniving at opium smuggling. This has occurred principally in the same Southern provinces where the rebellion commenced. It is almost needless to observe that, in the same measure in which opium has obtained the sovereignty over the Chinese, the Emperor and his staff of pedantic mandarins have become dispossessed of their own sovereignty. It would seem as though history had first to make this whole people drunk before it could rouse them out of their hereditary stupidity.

Though scarcely existing in former times, the import of English cottons, and to a small extent of English woollens, has rapidly risen since 1833, the epoch when the monopoly of trade with China was transferred from the East India Company to private commerce, and on a much greater scale since 1840, the epoch when other nations, and especially our own, also obtained a share in the Chinese trade. This introduction of foreign manufacturers has had a similar effect on the native industry to that which it formerly had on Asia Minor, Persia and India. In China the spinners and weavers have suffered greatly under this foreign competition, and the community has become unsettled in proportion.

The tribute to be paid to England after the unfortunate war of 1840, the great unproductive consumption of opium, the drain of the precious metals by this trade, the destructive influence of foreign competition on native manufactures, the demoralised condition of the public administration, produced two things: the old taxation became more burdensome and harassing, and new taxation was added to the old. Thus in a decree of the Emperor, dated Peking, Jan. 5, 1853, we find orders given to the viceroys and governors of the southern provinces of Wu-chang and Hang-Yang to remit and defer the payment of taxes, and especially not in any case to exact more than the regular amount; for otherwise, says the decree, 'how will the poor people be able to bear it?'

'And thus, perhaps,' continues the Emperor, 'will my people, in a period of general hardship and distress, be exempted from the evils of being pursued and worried by the tax-gatherer'.[2]

Such language as this, and such concessions we remember to have heard from Austria, the China of Germany, in 1848.

All these dissolving agencies acting together on the finances, the morals, the industry, and political structure of China, received their full development under the English cannon in 1840, which broke down the authority of the Emperor, and forced the Celestial Empire into contact with the terrestrial world. Complete isolation was the prime condition of the preservation of Old China. That isolation having come to a violent end by the medium of England, dissolution must follow as surely as that of any mummy carefully preserved in a hermetically sealed coffin, whenever it is brought into contact with the open air. Now, England having brought about the revolution of China, the question is how that revolution, will in time react on England, and through England on Europe. This question is not difficult of solution.

The attention of our readers has often been called to the unparalleled growth of British manufacturers since 1850. Amid the most surprising prosperity, it has not been difficult to point out the clear symptoms of an approaching industrial crisis. Notwithstanding California and Australia, notwithstanding the immense and unprecedented emigration, there must ever without any particular accident, in due time arrive a moment when the extension of the markets is unable to keep pace with the extension of British manufacturers, and this disproportion must bring about a new crisis with the same certainty as it has done in the past. But, if one of the great markets suddenly becomes contracted, the arrival of the crisis is necessarily accelerated thereby. Now, the Chinese rebellion must, for the time being, have precisely this effect upon England. The necessity for opening new markets, or for extending the old ones, was one of the principal causes of the reduction of the British tea-duties, as, with an increased importation of tea, an increased exportation of manufactures to China was expected to take place. Now, the value of the annual exports from the United Kingdom to China amounted, before the repeal in 1833 of the trading monopoly possessed by the East India Company, to only £600,000; in 1836, it reached the sum of £1,326,388; in 1845, it had risen to £2,394,827; in 1852, in amounted to about £3,000,000. The quantity of tea imported from China did not exceed, in 1793, 16,167,331 lbs; but in 1845, it amounted to 50,714,657 lbs; in 1846, to 57,584,561 lbs; it is now above 60,000,000 lbs.

The tea crop of the last season will not prove short, as shown already by the export lists from Shanghai, of 2,000,000 lbs above the preceding year. This excess is to be accounted for by two circumstances. On one hand, the state of the market at the close of 1851 was much depressed, and the large surplus stock left has been thrown into the export of 1852. On the other hand, the recent accounts of the altered British legislation with regard to imports of tea, reaching China, have brought forward all the available teas to a ready market, at greatly enhanced prices. But with respect to the coming crop, the case stands very differently. This is shown by the following extracts from the correspondence of a large tea-firm in London:

> In Shanghai the terror is extreme. Gold has advanced upward of 25 per cent, being eagerly sought for hoarding, silver has so far disappeared that

none could be obtained to pay the China dues on the British vessels requiring port clearance; and in consequence of which Mr Alcock has consented to become responsible to the Chinese authorities for the payment of these dues, on receipt of East India Company's bills, or other approved securities. *The scarcity of the precious metals* is one of the most unfavourable features, when viewed in reference to the immediate future of commerce, as this abstraction occurs precisely at that period when their use is most needed, to enable the tea and silk buyers to go into the interior and effect their purchases, for which a *large portion of bullion is paid in advance, to enable the producers to carry on their operations ...* At this period of the year it is usual to begin making arrangements for the new teas, whereas at present nothing is talked of but the means of protecting person and property, all transactions being at a stand ... If the means are not applied to secure the leaves in April and May, the early crop, which includes all the finer descriptions, both of black and green teas, will be as much lost as unreaped wheat at Christmas.[3]

Now the means for securing the tea leaves, will certainly not be given by the English, American or French squadrons stationed in the Chinese seas, but these may easily, by their interference, produce such complications, as to cut off all transactions between the tea-producing interior and the tea-exporting sea ports. Thus, for the present crop, a rise in the prices must be expected – speculation has already commenced in London – and for the crop to come a large deficit is as good as certain. Nor is this all. The Chinese, ready though they may be, as are all people in periods of revolutionary convulsion, to sell off to the foreigner all the bulky commodities they have on hand, will, as the Orientals are used to do in the apprehension of great changes, set to hoarding, not taking much in return for their tea and silk, except hard money. England has accordingly to expect a rise in the price of one of her chief articles of consumption, a drain of bullion, and a great contraction of an important market for her cotton and woollen goods. Even *The Economist*, that optimist conjuror of all things menacing the tranquil minds of the mercantile community, is compelled to use language like this:

> We must not flatter ourselves with finding as extensive a market for our exports to China as hitherto ... It is more probable that our export trade to China should suffer, and that there should be a diminished demand for the produce of Manchester and Glasgow.[4]

It must not be forgotten that the rise in the price of so indispensable an article as tea, and the contraction of so important a market as China, will coincide with a deficient harvest in Western Europe, and, therefore, with rising prices of meat, corn, and all other agricultural produce. Hence contracted markets for manufacturers, because every rise in the prices of the first necessaries of life is counterbalanced, at home and abroad, by a corresponding deduction in the demand for manufactures. From every part of Great Britain complaints have been received on the backward state of most of the crops. *The Economist* says on this subject:

> In the South of England not only will there be left much land unsown, until too late for a crop of any sort, but much of the sown land will prove to be foul, or otherwise in a bad state for corn-growing. On the wet or poor soils destined for wheat, signs that mischief is going on are apparent. The time for planting mangel-wurzel may now be said to have passed away, and very little has been planted, while the time for preparing land for the turnip is rapidly going by, without any adequate preparation for this important crop having been accomplished ... Oat-sowing has been much interfered with by the snow and rain. Few oats were sown early, and late sown oats seldom produce a large crop ... In many districts losses among the breeding flocks have been considerable.[5]

The price of other farm-produce than corn is from 20 to 30, and even 50 per cent higher than last year. On the Continent, corn has risen comparatively more than in England. Rye has risen in Belgium and Holland full 100 per cent. Wheat and other grains are following suit.

Under these circumstances, as the greater part of the regular commercial circle has already been run through by British trade, it may safely be augured that the Chinese revolution will throw the spark into the overloaded mine of the present industrial system and cause the explosion of the long-prepared general crisis, which, spreading abroad, will be closely followed by political revolutions on the Continent. It would be a curious spectacle, that of China sending disorder into the Western World while the Western powers, by English, French and American war-steamers, are conveying 'order' to Shanghai, Nanking, and the mouths of the Great Canal. Do these order-mongering powers, which would attempt to support the wavering Manchu dynasty, forget that the hatred against foreigners and their exclusion from the Empire, once the mere result of China's geographical and ethnographical situation, have become a political system only since the conquest of the country by the race of the Manchu Tartars? There can be no doubt that the turbulent dissensions among the European nations who, at the later end of the seventeenth century, rivalled each other in the trade with China, lent a mighty aid to the exclusive policy adopted by the Manchus. But more than this was done by the fear of the new dynasty, lest the foreigners might favour the discontent existing among a large proportion of the Chinese during the first half of the century or thereabouts of their subjection to the Tartars. From these considerations, foreigners were then prohibited from all communication with the Chinese, except through Canton, a town at a great distance from Peking and the tea-districts, and their commerce restricted to intercourse with the Hong merchants, licensed by the Government expressly for the foreign trade, in order to keep the rest of its subjects from all connection with the odious strangers. In any case an interference on the part of the Western Governments at this time can only serve to render the revolution more violent, and protract the stagnation of trade.

At the same time it is to be observed with regard to India, that the British Government of that country depends for full one seventh of its revenue on the sale of opium to the Chinese, while a considerable proportion of the Indian demand for British manufacturers depends on the production of that opium in India. The Chinese, it is true, are no more likely to renounce the use of opium than are the Germans to forswear tobacco. But as the new Emperor is understood to be favourable to the culture of the poppy and the preparation of opium in China itself, it is evident that a death-blow is very likely to be struck at once at the business of opium-raising in India, the Indian revenue, and the commercial resources of Hindostan. Though this blow would not immediately be felt by the interests concerned, it would operate effectually in due time, and would come in to intensify and prolong the universal financial crisis whose horoscope we have cast above.

Since the commencement of the eighteenth century there has been no serious revolution in Europe which had not been preceded by a commercial and financial crisis. This applies no less to the revolution of 1789 than to that of 1848. It is true, not only that we every day behold more threatening symptoms of conflict between the ruling powers and their subjects, between the State and society, between the various classes; but also the conflict of the existing powers among each other gradually reaching that height where the sword must be drawn, and the *ultima ratio* of princes be recurred to. In the European capitals, every day brings dispatches big with universal war, vanishing under the dispatches of the following day, bearing the assurance of peace for a week or so. We may be sure, nevertheless, that to whatever height the conflict between the European powers may rise, however threatening the aspect of the diplomatic horizon may appear, whatever movements may be attempted by some enthusiastic fraction in this or that country, the rage of princes and the fury of the people are alike enervated by the breath of prosperity. Neither wars nor revolutions are likely to put Europe by the ears, unless in consequence of a general commercial and industrial crisis, the signal of which has, as usual, to be given by England, the representative of European industry in the market of the world.

It is unnecessary to dwell on the political consequences such a crisis must produce in these times, with the unprecedented extension of factories in England, with the utter dissolution of her official parties, with the whole State machinery of France transformed into one immense swindling and stock-jobbing concern, with Austria on the eve of bankruptcy, with wrongs everywhere accumulated to be revenged by the people, with the conflicting interests of the reactionary powers themselves, and with the Russian dream of conquest once more revealed to the world.

Written on May 20-21, 1853
First published in the *New-York Daily Tribune*, No. 3794, June 14, 1853, as a Leader; reprinted in the *New-York Weekly Tribune*, No. 615, June 25, 1853
Reproduced from the *New-York Daily Tribune*

NOTES

1. Marx is referring to G.W.F. Hegel. [*Ed.*]
2. The Emperor Hxien Fêng quoted in the article 'China', *The Economist*, No. 505, April 30, 1853. [*Ed.*]
3. 'China and the Tea Trade', *The Economist*, No. 508, May 21, 1853. [*Ed.*]
4. *Ibid.* [*Ed.*]
5. 'Backwardness of the Season', *The Economist*, No. 507, May 14, 1853. [*Ed.*]

KARL MARX

THE FUTURE RESULTS OF BRITISH RULE IN INDIA

London, Friday, July 22,1853

I propose in this letter to conclude my observations on India.

How came it that English supremacy was established in India? The paramount power of the Great Mogul was broken by the Mogul Viceroys. The power of the Viceroys was broken by the Mahrattas. The power of the Mahrattas was broken by the Afghans, and while all were struggling against all, the Briton rushed in and was enabled to subdue them all. A country not only divided between Mahommedan and Hindoo, but between tribe and tribe, between caste and caste; a society whose framework was based on a sort of equilibrium, resulting from a general repulsion and constitutional exclusiveness between all its members. Such a country and such a society, were they not the predestined prey of conquest? If we knew nothing of the past history of Hindostan, would there not be the one great and incontestable fact, that even at this moment India is held in English thraldom by an Indian army maintained at the cost of India? India, then, could not escape the fate of being conquered, and the whole of her past history, if it be anything, is the history of the successive conquests she has undergone. Indian society has no history at all, at least no known history. What we call its history, is but the history of the successive intruders who founded their empires on the passive basis of that unresisting and unchanging society. The question, therefore, is not whether the English had a right to conquer India, but whether we are to prefer India conquered by the Turk, by the Persian, by the Russian, to India conquered by the Briton.

England has to fulfil a double mission in India: one destructive, the other regenerating – the annihilation of old Asiatic society, and the laying the material foundations of Western society in Asia.

Arabs, Turks, Tartars, Moguls, who had successively overrun India, soon became *Hindooized*, the barbarian conquerors being, by an eternal law of history, conquered themselves by the superior civilisation of their subjects. The British were the first conquerors superior, and therefore, inaccessible to Hindoo civilisation. They destroyed it by breaking up the native communities, by uprooting the native industry, and by levelling all that was great and elevated in the native society. The historic pages of their rule in India report hardly anything beyond that destruction. The work of regeneration hardly transpired through a heap of ruins. Nevertheless it has begun.

The political unity of India, more consolidated, and extending farther than it ever did under the Great Moguls, was the first condition of its regeneration. That unity, imposed by the British sword, will now be strengthened and perpetuated by the electric telegraph. The native army, organised and trained by the British drill-sergeant, was the *sine qua non* of Indian self-emancipation, and of India ceasing to be the prey of the first foreign intruder. The free press, introduced for the first time into Asiatic society, and managed principally by the common offspring of Hindoos and Europeans, is a new and powerful agent of reconstruction. The Zemindari and Ryotwar themselves, abominable as they are, involve two distinct forms of private property in land – the great desideratum of Asiatic society. From the Indian natives, reluctantly and sparingly educated at Calcutta, under English superintendence, a fresh class is springing up, endowed with the requirements for government and imbued with European science. Steam has brought India into regular and rapid communication with Europe, has connected its chief ports with those of the whole south-eastern ocean, and has revindicated it from the isolated position which was the prime law of its stagnation. The day is not far distant when, by a combination of railways and steam-vessels, the distance between England and India, measured by time, will be shortened to eight days, and when that once fabulous country will thus be actually annexed to the Western world.

The ruling classes of Great Britain have had, till now, but an accidental, transitory and exceptional interest in the progress of India. The aristocracy wanted to conquer it, the moneyocracy to plunder it, and the millocracy to undersell it. But now the tables are turned. The millocracy have discovered that the transformation of India into a reproductive country has become of vital importance to them, and that, to that end, it is necessary, above all, to gift her with means of irrigation and of internal communication. They intend now drawing a net of railroads over India. And they will do it. The results must be inappreciable.

It is notorious that the productive powers of India are paralysed by the utter want of means for conveying and exchanging its various produce. Nowhere, more than in India, do we meet with social destitution in the midst of natural plenty, for want of the means of exchange. It was proved before a Committee of the British House of Commons, which sat in 1848, that

> when grain was selling from 6/ to 8/ a quarter at Khandesh, it was sold at 64/ to 70/ at Poona, where the people were dying in the streets of famine, without the possibility of gaining supplies from Khandesh, because the clay-roads were impracticable.[1]

The introduction of railroads may be easily made to subserve agricultural purposes by the formation of tanks, where ground is required for embankment, and by the conveyance of water along the different lines. Thus irrigation, the *sine qua non* of farming in the East, might be greatly extended, and the frequently recurring local famines, arising from the want of water, would be averted. The general importance of railways, viewed under this head, must become evident, when we remember that irrigated lands, even in the districts near Ghauts, pay three times as much in taxes, afford ten or twelve times as much employment, and yield twelve or fifteen times as much profit, as the same area without irrigation.

Railways will afford the means of diminishing the amount and the cost of the military establishments. Col. Warren, Town Major of the

Fort St William, stated before a Select Committee of the House of Commons:

> The practicability of receiving intelligence from distant parts of the country, in as many hours as at present it requires days and even weeks, and of sending instructions, with troops and stores, in the more brief period, are considerations which cannot be too highly estimated. Troops could be kept at more distant and healthier stations than at present, and much loss of life from sickness would by this means be spared. Stores could not to the same extent be required at the various dépôts, and the loss by decay, and the destruction incidental to the climate, would also be avoided. The number of troops might be diminished in direct proportion to their effectiveness.

We know that the municipal organisation and the economical basis of the village communities has been broken up, but their worst feature, the dissolution of society into stereotype and disconnected atoms, has survived their vitality. The village isolation produced the absence of roads in India, and the absence of roads perpetuated the village isolation. On this plan a community existed with a given scale of low conveniences, almost without intercourse with other villages, without the desires and efforts indispensable to social advance. The British having broken up this self-sufficient *inertia* of the villages, railways will provide the new want of communication and intercourse. Besides,

> one of the effects of the railway system will be to bring into every village affected by it such knowledge of the contrivances and appliances of other countries, and such means of obtaining them, as will first put the hereditary and stipendiary village artisanship of India to full proof of its capabilities, and then supply its defects.[2]

I know that the English millocracy intend to endow India with railways with the exclusive view of extracting at diminished expenses the cotton and other raw materials for their manufactures. But when you have once introduced machinery into the locomotion of a country, which possess iron and coals, you are unable to withhold it from its fabrication. You cannot maintain a net of railways over an immense country without introducing all those industrial processes necessary to meet the immediate and current wants of railway locomotion, and out of which there must grow the application of machinery to those branches of industry not immediately connected with railways. The railway-system will therefore become, in India, truly the forerunner of modern industry. This is more certain as the Hindoos are allowed by British authorities themselves to possess particular aptitude for accommodating themselves to entirely new labour, and acquiring the requisite knowledge of machinery. Ample proof of this fact is afforded by the capacities and expertness of the native engineers in the Calcutta mint, where they have been for years employed in working the steam machinery, by the natives attached to the several steam engines in the Burdwan coal districts, and by other instances. Mr Campbell himself, greatly influenced as he is by the prejudices of the East India Company, is obliged to avow

> that the great mass of the Indian people possesses a great industrial energy, is well fitted to accumulate capital, and remarkable for a mathematical clearness of head, and talent for figures and exact sciences. 'Their intellects,' he says, 'are excellent'.[3]

Modern industry, resulting from the railway system, will dissolve the hereditary divisions of labour, upon which rest the Indian castes, those decisive impediments to Indian progress and Indian power.

All the English bourgeoisie may be forced to do will neither emancipate nor materially mend the social condition of the mass of the people, depending not only on the development of the productive powers, but on their appropriation by the people. But what they will not fail to do is to lay down the material premises for both. Has the bourgeoisie ever done more? Has it ever effected a progress without dragging individuals and people through blood and dirt, through misery and degradation?

The Indians will not reap the fruits of the new elements of society scattered among them by the British bourgeoisie, till in Great Britain itself the now ruling classes shall have been supplanted by the industrial proletariat, or till the Hindoos themselves shall have grown strong enough to throw off the English yoke altogether. At all events, we may safely expect to see, at a more or less remote period, the regeneration of that great and interesting country, whose gentle natives are, to use the expression of Prince Soltykov, even in the most inferior classes, *'plus fins et plus adroits que les Italiens,'*[4] whose submission even is counterbalanced by a certain calm nobility, who, notwithstanding their natural languor, have astonished the British officers by their bravery, whose country has been the source of our languages, our religions, and who represent the type of the ancient German in the Jat, and the type of the ancient Greek in the Brahmin.

I cannot part with the subject of India without some concluding remarks.

The profound hypocrisy and inherent barbarism of bourgeois civilisation lies unveiled before our eyes, turning from its home, where it assumes respectable forms, to the colonies, where it goes naked. They are the defenders of property, but did any revolutionary party ever originate agrarian revolutions like those in Bengal, in Madras, and in Bombay? Did they not, in India, to borrow an expression of that great robber, Lord Clive himself, resort to atrocious extortion, when simple corruption could not keep pace with their rapacity? While they prated in Europe about the inviolable sanctity of the national debt, did they not confiscate in India the dividends of the rajahs, who had invested their private savings in the Company's own funds? While they combatted the French revolution under the pretext of defending 'our holy religion', did they not forbid, at the same time, Christianity to be propagated in India, and did they not, in order to make money out of the pilgrims streaming to the temples of Orissa and Bengal, take up the trade in the murder and prostitution perpetrated in the temple of Juggernaut? These are the men of 'Property, Order, Family, and Religion'.

The devastating effects of English industry, when contemplated with regard to India, a country as vast as Europe, and containing 150 millions of acres, are palpable and confounding. But we must not forget that they are only the organic results of the whole system of production as it is now constituted. That production rests on the supreme rule of capital. The centralisation of capital is essential to the existence of capital as an independent power. The destructive influence of that centralisation upon the markets of the world does but reveal, in the most gigantic dimensions, the inherent organic laws of political economy now at work in every civilised town. The bourgeois period of history has to create the material basis of the new world – on the one hand universal intercourse founded upon the mutual dependency of mankind, and the means of that intercourse; on the other hand the development of the productive powers of man and the transformation of material production into a scientific domination of material conditions of a new world in the same way as geological revolutions have created the surface of the earth. When a great social revolution shall have mastered the results of the bourgeois epoch, the market of the world and the modern powers of production, and subjected them to the common control of the most advanced peoples, then only will human progress cease to resemble that hideous, pagan idol, who would not drink the nectar but from the skulls of the slain.

Written on July 22, 1853
First published in the *New-York Daily Tribune*, No. 3840, August 8, 1853; re-printed in the *New-York Semi-Weekly Tribune*, No. 856, August 9, 1853
Signed: *Karl Marx*
Reproduced from the *New-York Daily Tribune*

NOTES
1. Quoted from J. Dickinson's *The Government of India under a Bureaucracy*, pp81-82. [*Ed.*]
2. Chapman, *The Cotton and Commerce of India*, pp95-97.
3. G. Campbell, *Modern India: a Sketch of the System of Civil Government*, pp59-60. [*Ed.*]
4. 'More subtle and adroit than the Italians,' See A.D. Soltykov's *Lettres sur l'Inde*, p61. [*Ed.*]

10

KARL MARX
THE INDIAN REVOLT

London, Sept. 4, 1857

The outrages committed by the revolted Sepoys in India are indeed appalling, hideous, ineffable – such as one is prepared to meet only in wars of insurrection, of nationalities, of races, and above all of religion; in one word, such as respectable England used to applaud when perpetrated by the Vendeans on the 'Blues', by the Spanish guerrillas on the infidel Frenchmen, by Servians on their German and Hungarian neighbours, by Croats on Viennese rebels, by Cavaignac's Garde Mobile or Bonaparte's Decembrists on the sons and daughters of proletarian France. However infamous the conduct of the Sepoys, it is only the reflex, in a concentrated form, of England's own conduct in India, not only during the epoch of the foundation of her Eastern Empire, but even during the last ten years of a long-settled rule. To characterise that rule, it suffices to say that torture formed an organic institution of its financial policy. There is something in human history like retribution; and it is a rule of historical retribution that its instrument be forged not by the offended, but by the offender himself.

The first blow dealt to the French monarchy proceeded from the nobility, not from the peasants. The Indian revolt does not commence with the Ryots, tortured, dishonoured and stripped naked by the British, but with the Sepoys, clad, fed, petted, fatted and pampered by them. To find parallels to the Sepoy atrocities, we need not, as some London papers pretend, fall back on the middle ages, nor even wander beyond the history of contemporary England. All we want is to study the first Chinese war, an event, so to say, of yesterday. The English soldiery then committed abominations for the mere fun of it; their passions being neither sanctified by religious fanaticism nor exacerbated by hatred against an overbearing and conquering race, nor provoked by the stern resistance of a heroic enemy. The violations of women, the spittings of children, the roastings of whole villages, were then mere wanton sports, not recorded by Mandarins, but by British officers themselves.

Even at the present catastrophe it would be an unmitigated mistake to suppose that all the cruelty is on the side of the Sepoys, and all the milk of human kindness flows on the side of the English. The letters of the British officers are redolent of malignity. An officer writing from Peshawur gives a description of the disarming of the 10th irregular cavalry for not charging the 55th native infantry when ordered to do so. He exults in the fact that they were not only disarmed, but stripped of their coats and boots, and after having received 12d. per man, were marched down to the river side, and there embarked in boats and sent down the Indus, where the writer is delighted to expect every mother's son will have a chance of being drowned in the rapids. Another writer informs us that, some inhabitants of Peshawur having caused a night alarm by exploding little mines of gunpowder in honour of a wedding (a national custom), the persons concerned were tied up next morning, and

received such a flogging as they will not easily forget.

News arrived from Pindee that three native chiefs were plotting. Sir John Lawrence replied by a message ordering a spy to attend to the meeting. On the spy's report, Sir John sent a second message, 'Hang them.' The chiefs were hanged.[1] An officer in the civil service, from Allahabad, writes:

We have power of life and death in our hands, and we assure you we spare not.[2]

Another, from the same place:

Not a day passes but we string up from ten to fifteen of them (non-combatants).

98

One exulting officer writes:

> Holmes is hanging them by the score, like a 'brick'.[3]

Another, in allusion to the summary hanging of a large body of natives:

> Then our fun commenced.

A third:

> We hold court-martials on horseback, and every nigger we meet with we either string up or shoot.

From Benares we are informed that thirty Zemindars were hanged on the mere suspicion of sympathising with their own countrymen, and whole villages were burned down on the same plea. An officer from Benares, whose letter is printed in *The London Times*, says:

> The European troops have become fiends when opposed to natives.[4]

And then it should not be forgotten that, while the cruelties of the English are related as acts of martial vigour, told simply, rapidly, without dwelling on disgusting details, the outrages of the natives, shocking as they are, are still deliberately exaggerated. For instance, the circumstantial account first appearing in *The Times*, and then going the round of the London press, of the atrocities perpetrated at Delhi and Meerut, from whom did it proceed?[5] From a cowardly parson residing at Bangalore, Mysore, more than a thousand miles, as the bird flies, distant from the scene of action. Actual accounts of Delhi evince the imagination of an English parson to be capable of breeding greater horrors than even the wild fancy of a Hindoo mutineer. The cutting of noses, breasts, &c., in one word, the horrid mutilations committed by the Sepoys, are of course more revolting to European feeling than the throwing of red-hot shell on Canton dwellings by a Secretary of the Manchester Peace Society,[6] or the roasting of Arabs pent up in a cave by a French Marshal, or the flaying alive of British soldiers by the cat-o'-nine-tails under drum-head court-martial, or any other of the philanthropical appliances used in British penitentiary colonies. Cruelty, like every other thing, has its fashion, changing according to time and place. Caesar, the accomplished scholar, candidly narrates how he ordered many thousand Gallic warriors to have their right hand cut off.[7] Napoleon would have been ashamed to do this. He preferred dispatching his own French regiments, suspected of republicanism, to St Domingo, there to die of the blacks and the plague.

The infamous mutilations committed by the Sepoys remind one of the practices of the Christian Byzantine Empire, or the prescriptions of Emperor Charles V's criminal law, or the English punishments for high treason, as still recorded by Judge Blackstone.[8] With Hindoos, whom their religion has made virtuosi in the art of self-torturing, these tortures inflicted on the enemies of their race and creed appear quite natural, and must appear still more so to the English, who, only some years since, still used to draw revenues from the Juggernaut festivals, protecting and assisting the bloody rites of a religion of cruelty.

The frantic roars of the 'bloody old *Times*', as Cobbett used to call it – its playing the part of a furious character in one of Mozart's operas, who indulges in most melodious strains in the idea of first hanging his enemy, then roasting him, then quartering him, then spitting him, and then flaying him alive[9] – its tearing the passion of revenge to tatters and to rags – all this would appear but silly if under the pathos of tragedy there were not distinctly perceptible the tricks of comedy. *The London Times* overdoes its part, not only from panic. It supplies comedy with a subject even missed by Molière, the Tartuffe of Revenge. What it simply wants is to write up the funds and to screen the Government. As Delhi has not, like the walls of Jericho, fallen before mere puffs of wind, John Bull is to be steeped in cries for revenge up to his very ears, to make him forget that his Government is responsible for the mischief hatched and the colossal dimensions it has been allowed to assume.

Written on September 4, 1857
First published unsigned in the *New-York Daily Tribune*, No. 5119,
September 16, 1857
Reproduced from the newspaper

NOTES

1. From a letter of an artillery officer, dated Peshawur, June 26, *The Times*, No. 22766, August 22, 1857. [*Ed.*]
2. 'Allahabad, June 28', *The Times*, No. 22768, August 25, 1857. [*Ed.*]
3. Letter from Tirhoot, dated June 26, *The Times*, No. 22763, August 19, 1857. [*Ed.*]
4. R.H. Bartrum, 'Benares, July 13'. *The Times*, No. 22775, September 2, 1857. [*Ed.*]
5. 'Bangalore, July 4', *The Times*, No. 22768, August 25, 1857. [*Ed.*]
6. John Bowring, (A letter to Consul Parkes of October 11, 1856), in 'The Bombardment of Canton', *The Times*, No. 22571, January 7, 1857. [*Ed.*]
7. Gaius Julius Caesar, *Commentarii de bello Callico*, Libr VIII, cap. XLIV. [*Ed.*]
8. W. Blackstone, *Commentaries on the Laws of England*. [*Ed.*]
9. W.A. Mozart, *Die Entführung aus dem Serail*, Act III, Scene 6, Osmin's aria. [*Ed.*]

Section 5: Technological determinism

11. Karl Marx, 'Theses on Feuerbach' (1845), *Marx and Engels Collected Works*, vol. 5, pp3-5

12. Karl Marx, 'Second Observation', from *The Poverty of Philosophy* (1847), *Marx and Engels Collected Works*, vol. 6, pp165-166

One of the most popular readings of Marx used to describe his philosophy as a form of economic (or sometimes technological) determinism. As production grew, so society changed. The economic base of society formed the structure, out of which ideas, art, philosophy and culture all grew. Whether Marx was actually a 'structuralist' remains a moot point, but a similar determinism seems to inform many supporters of the globalisation argument, when they maintain that the spread of new forms of industry (typically, information technology) must by definition transform the world.

The extracts here suggest that Marx was not a determinist. He approached these questions from a background in the philosophical debates of the early 1840s. The young enthusiasts of the time attempted to apply Hegel's philosophy, which stressed the inevitability of change, to social affairs. The freethinker Ludwig Feuerbach was one of the most prominent 'Young Hegelians'. The 'Theses on Feuerbach' were jotted down early in Marx's life, as an attempt to make sense of his approach. Feuerbach maintained that people's lives were entirely determined by their environment, 'man is what he eats'. Marx's counter-argument, that human practice transforms the world, is expressed up in the final thesis, 'The philosophers have only interpreted the world in various ways; the point is to change it'.

The second extract comes from *The Poverty of Philosophy*, Marx's polemic against the French socialist Pierre-Joseph Proudhon. Marx wrote seven 'observations' on Proudhon's philosophy, which he believed was hopelessly crude compared to the dialectical method of Hegel. This passage again stresses the role of human agency – people are not merely prisoners of circumstances, but contribute to the shaping of their world.

11

KARL MARX
[THESES ON FEUERBACH]

1

The chief defect of all previous materialism (that of Feuerbach included) is that things [*Gegenstand*], reality, sensuousness are conceived only in the form of the *object, or of contemplation*, but not as *sensuous human activity, practice*, not subjectively. Hence, in contradistinction to materialism, the *active* side was set forth abstractly by idealism – which, of course, does not know real, sensuous activity as such. Feuerbach wants sensuous objects, really distinct from conceptual objects, but he does not conceive human activity itself as *objective* activity. In *Das Wesen des Christenthums*, he therefore regards the theoretical attitude as the only genuinely human attitude, while practice is conceived and defined only in its dirty-Jewish form of appearance. Hence he does not grasp the significance of 'revolutionary', of 'practical-critical', activity.

2

The question whether objective truth can be attributed to human thinking is not a question of theory but is a *practical* question. Man must prove the truth, i.e., the reality and power, the this-worldliness of his thinking in practice. The dispute over the reality or non-reality of thinking which is isolated from practice is a purely *scholastic* question.

3

The materialist doctrine concerning the changing of circumstances and upbringing forgets that circumstances are changed by men and that the educator must himself be educated. This doctrine must, therefore, divide society into two parts, one of which is superior to society.

The coincidence of the changing of circumstances and of human activity or self-change can be conceived and rationally understood only as *revolutionary practice*.

4

Feuerbach starts out from the fact of religious self-estrangement, of the duplication of the world into a religious world and a secular one. His work consists in resolving the religious world into its secular basis. But that the secular basis lifts off from itself and establishes itself as an independent realm in the clouds can only be explained by the inner strife and intrinsic contradictoriness of this secular basis. The latter must, therefore, itself be both understood in its contradiction and revolutionised in practice. Thus, for instance, once the earthly family is discovered to be the secret of the holy family, the former must then itself be destroyed in theory and in practice.

5

Feuerbach, not satisfied with *abstract thinking*, wants [*sensuous*] *contemplation*; but he does not conceive sensuousness as *practical*, human-sensuous activity.

6

Feuerbach resolves the essence of religion into the essence of *man*. But the essence of man is no abstraction inherent in each single individual. In its reality it is the ensemble of the social relations.

Feuerbach, who does not enter upon a criticism of this real essence, is hence obliged:

1. To abstract from the historical process and to define the religious sentiment [*Gemüt*] by itself, and to presuppose an abstract – *isolated*- human individual.

2. Essence, therefore, can be regarded only as 'species', as an inner, mute, general character which unites the many individuals *in a natural way*.

7

Feuerbach, consequently, does not see that the 'religious sentiment' is itself a social product, and that the abstract individual which he analyses belongs to a particular form of society.

8

All social life is essentially *practical*. All mysteries which lead theory to mysticism find their rational solution in human practice and in the comprehension of this practice.

9

The highest point reached by contemplative materialism, that is, materialism which does not comprehend sensuousness as practical activity, is the contemplation of single individuals and of civil society.

10

The standpoint of the old materialism is civil society; the standpoint of the new is human society, or social humanity.

11

The philosophers have only *interpreted* the world in various ways; the point is to *change* it.

Written in the spring of 1845
This version was first published in 1924 – in German and in Russian – by the Institute of Marxism-Leninism of the Central Committee of the C.P.S.U. in *Marx-Engels Archives*, Book I, Moscow
Printed according to the manuscript.

12

SECOND OBSERVATION

Economic categories are only the theoretical expressions, the abstractions of the social relations of production. M. Proudhon holding things upside down like a true philosopher, sees in actual relations nothing but the incarnation of these principles, of these categories, which were slumbering – so, M. Proudhon the philosopher tells us – in the bosom of the 'impersonal reason of humanity'.

M. Proudhon the economist understands very well that men make cloth, linen or silk materials in definite relations of production. But what he has not understood is that these definite social relations are just as much produced by men as linen, flax, etc. Social relations are closely bound up with productive forces. In acquiring new productive forces men change their mode of production; and in changing their mode of production, in changing the way of earning their living, they change all their social relations. The hand-mill gives you society with the feudal lord; the steam-mill, society with the industrial capitalist.

The same men who establish their social relations in conformity with their material productivity, produce also principles, ideas and categories, in conformity with their social relations.

Thus these ideas, these categories, are as little eternal as the relations they express. They are *historical and transitory products*.

There is a continual movement of growth in productive forces, of destruction in social relations, of formation in ideas; the only immutable thing is the abstraction of movement – *mors immortalis*.[1]

NOTE
1. These words are from Lucretius' poem *On the Nature of Things*, Book III, line 882 ('mortalem vitam mors immortalis alemit' – 'mortal life has been usurped by death the immortal'). [*Ed.*]

Section 6: Commodities and consumerism

Associated with the globalisation argument stands the claim that work is becoming less important, and consumption more decisive in shaping people's lives. Sometimes, this claim can be very optimistic – as with the notion that people are liberated, now that we can purchase goods anywhere in the world, over the internet. At other times, this globalisation of desire is seen as a human loss. Most writers describe the spread of corporate logos in every country as the destruction of local tastes. The new citizens of anti-corporatism used the huge protests at Seattle in 1999 to attack the Starbucks coffee chain, the equivalent protesters in London six months later chose fast-food chain MacDonalds for their target.

Two of the passages in this section come from Marx's early notes on economics, the third from an article published in the German press in the 1860s. Each of these three passages discusses the theme of consumption, and asks whether people can find liberation in this sphere? The first discusses alienation, or to use Marx's synonyms, 'objectification' and 'estrangement'. Here Marx argues that human nature is defined by our capacity to work. No other species can transform the world to the extent that humans can. Having stressed the importance of labour in all human life, Marx went on to argue that under capitalism work was miserable. People did not choose their work, they did not control it. So Marx claimed that alienation experienced at the workplace tended to shape every other sphere of life. People could not be free at home, if they spent eight hours of the day tied to a machine.

The second extract deals with the nature of money. As with the first extract in this section, this passage is from Karl Marx's 1844 *Economic and Philosophical Manuscripts*. Marx was just twenty-six when he compiled these notes. Many of the authorities cited come from literature – including Shakespeare's play *Timon of Athens*. Marx concludes that money is the very negation of what it means to be human, 'the alienated ability of mankind'. Indeed there is a rare sensuousness about Marx's attack here on the effect of money to reduce human freedom.

The third extract is a rarely-cited passage on bread manufacture in England. Marx was astonished that new and cleaner methods of food production were being held back, lest they jeopardised the profits of the larger companies. This failing Karl Marx described as symptomatic. Far from seeking the market as a potential source of freedom, Marx saw consumption as another fetter, another obstacle to human aspiration. People could not shop their way to freedom.

13

[ESTRANGED LABOUR]

[XXII] We have proceeded from the premises of political economy. We have accepted its language and its laws. We presupposed private property, the separation of labour, capital and land, and of wages, profit of capital and rent of land – likewise division of labour, competition, the concept of exchange-value, etc. On the basis of political economy itself, in its own words, we have shown that the worker sinks to the level of a commodity and becomes indeed the most wretched of commodities; that the wretchedness of the worker is in inverse proportion to the power and magnitude of his production; that the necessary result of competition is the accumulation of capital in a few hands, and thus the restoration of monopoly in a more terrible form; and that finally the distinction between capitalist and land rentier, like that between the tiller of the soil and the factory worker, disappears and that the whole of society must fall apart into the two classes – the *property owners* and the propertyless *workers*.

Political economy starts with the fact of private property; it does not explain it to us. It expresses in general, abstract formulas the *material* process through which private property actually passes, and these formulas it then takes for *laws* does not *comprehend* these laws, i.e., it does not demonstrate how they arise from the very nature of private property. Political economy throws no light on the cause of the division between labour and capital, and between capital and land. When, for example, it defines the relationship of wages to profit, it takes the interest of the capitalists to be the ultimate cause, i.e., it takes for granted what it is supposed to explain. Similarly, competition comes in everywhere. It is explained from external circumstances. As to how far these external and apparently accidental circumstances are but the expression of a necessary course of development, political economy teaches us nothing. We have seen how exchange itself appears to it as an accidental fact. The only wheels which political economy sets in motion are *greed* and the *war amongst the greedy – competition.*

Precisely because political economy does not grasp the way the movement is connected, it was possible to oppose, for instance, the doctrine of competition to the doctrine of monopoly, the doctrine of the freedom of the crafts to the doctrine of the guild, the doctrine of the division of landed property to the doctrine of the big estate – for competition, freedom of the crafts and the division of landed property were explained and comprehended only as accidental, premeditated and violent consequences of monopoly, of the guild system, and of feudal property, not as their necessary, inevitable and natural consequences.

Now, therefore, we have to grasp the intrinsic connection between private property, avarice, the separation of labour, capital and landed property; the connection of exchange and competition, of value and the devaluation of men, of monopoly and competition, etc. – we have to grasp this whole estrangement connected with the *money* system.

Do not let us go back to a fictitious primordial condition as the political economist does, when he tries to explain. Such a primordial condition explains nothing; it merely pushes the question away into a grey nebulous distance. The economist assumes in the form of a fact, of an event, what he is supposed to deduce – namely, the necessary relationship between two things – between, for example, division of labour and exchange. Thus the theologian explains the origin of evil by the fall of man; that is, he assumes as a fact, in historical form, what has to be explained.

We proceed from an *actual* economic fact.

The worker becomes all the poorer the more wealth he produces, the more his production increases in power and size. The worker becomes an ever cheaper commodity the more commodities he creates. The *devaluation* of the world of men is in direct proportion to the *increasing value* of the world of things. Labour produces not only commodities: it produces itself and the worker as a *commodity* – and this at the same rate at which it produces commodities in general.

This fact expresses merely that the object which labour produces –

labour's product – confronts it as *something alien*, as a *power independent* of the producer. The product of labour is labour which has been embodied in an object, which has become material: it is the *objectification* of labour. Labour's realisation is its objectification. Under these economic conditions this realisation of labour appears as *loss of realisation* for the workers; objectification as *loss of the object and bondage to it*; appropriation as *estrangement, as alienation*.

So much does labour's realisation appear as loss of realisation that the worker loses realisation to the point of starving to death. So much does objectification appear as loss of the object that the worker is robbed of the objects most necessary not only for his life but for his work. Indeed, labour itself becomes an object which he can obtain only with the greatest effort and with the most irregular interruptions. So much does the appropriation of the object appear as estrangement that the more objects the worker produces the less he can possess and the more he falls under the sway of his product, capital.

All these consequences are implied in the statement that the worker is related to the *product of his labour* as to an *alien* object. For on this premise it is clear that the more the worker spends himself, the more powerful becomes the alien world of objects which he creates over and against himself, the poorer he himself – his inner world – becomes, the less belongs to him as his own. It is the same in religion. The more man puts into God, the less he retains in himself. The worker puts his life into the object; but now his life no longer belongs to him but to the object. Hence, the greater this activity, the more the worker lacks objects. Whatever the product of his labour is, he is not. Therefore the greater this product, the less is he himself. The *alienation* of the worker in his product means not only that his labour becomes an object, an *external* existence, but that it exists *outside him*, independently, as something alien to him, and that it becomes a power on its own confronting him. It means that the life which he has conferred on the object confronts him as something hostile and alien.

[XXIII] Let us now look more closely at the *objectification*, at the production of the worker; and in it at the *estrangement*, the loss of the object, of his product.

The worker can create nothing without *nature*, without the *sensuous external world*. It is the material on which his labour is realised, in which it is active, from which and by means of which it produces.

But just as nature provides labour with [the] *means of life* in the sense that labour cannot *live* without objects on which to operate, on the other hand, it also provides the *means of life* in the more restricted sense, i.e., the means for the physical subsistence of the *worker* himself.

Thus the more the worker by his labour *appropriates* the external world, sensuous nature, the more he deprives himself of *means of life* in two respects: first, in that the sensuous external world more and more ceases to be an object belonging to his labour – to be his labour's *means of life*; and secondly, in that it more and more ceases to be *means of life* in the immediate sense, means for the physical subsistence of the worker.

In both respects, therefore, the worker becomes a servant of his object, first, in that he receives an *object of labour* i.e., in that he receives *work*; and secondly, in that he receives *means of subsistence*. This enables him to exist, first, as a *worker*, and, second, as a *physical subject*. The height of this servitude is that it is only as a *worker* that he can maintain himself as a *physical subject*, and that it is only as a *physical subject* that he is a worker.

(According to the economic laws the estrangement of the worker in his object is expressed thus: the more the worker produces, the less he has to consume; the more values he creates, the more valueless, the more unworthy he becomes; the better formed his product, the more deformed becomes the worker; the more civilised his object, the more barbarous becomes the worker; the more powerful labour becomes, the more powerless becomes the worker; the more ingenious labour becomes, the less ingenious becomes the worker and the more he becomes nature's servant.)

Political economy conceals the estrangement inherent in the nature of labour by not considering the direct *relationship between the* worker (labour) *and production.* It is true that labour produces wonderful things for the rich – but for the worker it produces privation. It produces palaces – but for the worker, hovels. It produces beauty – but for the worker, deformity. It replaces labour by machines, but it throws one section of the workers back to a barbarous type of labour, and it turns the other section into a machine. It produces intelligence – but for the worker, stupidity, cretinism.

The direct relationship of labour to its products is the relationship of the worker to the objects of his production. The relationship of the man of means to the objects of production and to production itself is only a *consequence* of this first relationship – and confirms it. We shall consider this other aspect later. When we ask, then, what is the essential relationship of labour we are asking about the relationship of the *worker*. To production.

Till now we have been considering the estrangement, the alienation of the worker only in one of its aspects, i.e., the worker's *relationship to the products of his labour*. But the estrangement is manifested not only in the result but in the *act of production*, within the *producing activity* itself. How could the worker come to face the product of his activity as a stranger, were it not that in the very act of production he was estranging himself from himself? The product is after all but the summary of the activity, of production. If then the product of labour is alienation, production itself must be active alienation, the alienation of activity, the activity of alienation. In the estrangement of the object of labour is merely summarised the estrangement, the alienation, in the activity of labour itself.

What, then, constitutes the alienation of labour?

First, the fact that labour is *external* to the worker, i.e., it does not belong to his intrinsic nature; that in his work, therefore, he does not affirm himself but denies himself, does not feel content but unhappy, does not develop freely his physical and mental energy but mortifies his body and ruins his mind. The worker therefore only feels himself outside his work, and in his work feels outside himself. He feels at home when he is not working, and when he is working he does not feel at home. His labour is therefore not voluntary, but coerced; it is *forced labour*. It is therefore not the satisfaction of a need; it is merely a *means* to satisfy needs external to it. Its alien character emerges clearly in the fact that as soon as no physical or other compulsion exists, labour is shunned like the plague. External labour, labour in which man alienates himself, is a labour of self-sacrifice, of mortification. Lastly, the external character of labour for the worker appears in the fact that it is not his own, but someone else's, that it does not belong to him, that in it he belongs, not to himself, but to another. Just as in religion the spontaneous activity of the human imagination, of the human brain and the human heart, operates on the individual independently of him – that is, operates as an alien, divine or diabolical activity – so is the worker's activity not his spontaneous activity. It belongs to another; it is the loss of his self.

As a result, therefore, man (the worker) only feels himself freely active in his animal functions – eating, drinking, procreating, or at most in his dwelling and in dressing-up, etc.; and in his human functions he no longer feels himself to be anything but an animal. What is animal becomes human and what is human becomes animal.

Certainly eating, drinking, procreating, etc., are also genuinely human functions. But taken abstractly, separated from the sphere of all other human activity and turned into sole and ultimate ends, they are animal functions.

We have considered the act of estranging practical human activity, labour, in two of its aspects. (1) The relation of the worker to the *product of labour* as an alien object exercising power over him. This relation is at the same time the relation to the sensuous external world, to the objects of nature, as an alien world inimically opposed to him. (2) The relation of labour to the *act of production* within the *labour* process. This relation is the relation of the worker to his own activity as an alien activity not belonging to him; it is activity as suffering, strength as weakness, begetting as emasculating, the worker's *own* physical and mental energy, his personal life – for what is life but activity? – as an activity which is turned against him, independent of him and not belonging to him. Here we have *self-estrangement*, as previously we had the estrangement of the *thing*.

[XXIV] We have still a third aspect of *estranged labour* to deduce from the two already considered.

Man is a species-being, not only because in practice and in theory he adopts the species (his own as well as those of other things) as his object, but – and this is only another way of expressing it – also because he treats himself as the actual, living species; because he treats himself as a *universal* and therefore a free being.

The life of the species, both in man and in animals, consists physically in the fact that man (like the animal) lives on inorganic nature; and the more universal man (or the animal) is, the more universal is the sphere of inorganic nature on which he lives. Just as plants, animals, stones, air, light, etc., constitute theoretically a part of human consciousness, partly as objects of natural science, partly as objects of art – his spiritual inorganic nature, spiritual nourishment which he must first prepare to make palatable and digestible – so also the realm of practice they constitute a part of human life and human activity. Physically man lives only on these products of nature, whether they appear in the form of food, heating, clothes, a dwelling, etc. The universality of man appears in practice precisely in the universality which makes all nature his *inorganic* body – both inasmuch as nature is (1) his direct means of life, and (2) the material, the object, and the instrument of his life activity. Nature is man's *inorganic body* - nature, that is, insofar as it is not itself human body. Man *lives* on nature – means that nature is his *body*, with which he must remain in continuous interchange if he is not to die. That man's physical and spiritual life is linked to nature means simply that nature is linked to itself, for man is a part of nature.

In estranging from man (1) nature, and (2) himself, his own active functions, his life activity, estranged labour estranges the *species* from man. It changes for him the *life of the species* into a means of individual life. First it estranges the life of the species and individual life, and secondly it makes individual life in its abstract form the purpose of the life of the species, likewise in its abstract and estranged form.

For labour, *life activity, productive life* itself, appears to man in the first place merely as a *means* of satisfying a need – the need to maintain physical existence. Yet the productive life is the life of the species. It is life-engendering life. The whole character of a species – its species-character – is contained in the character of its life activity; and free, conscious activity is man's species-character. Life itself appears only as a *means to life*.

The animal is immediately one with its life activity. It does not distinguish itself from it. It is *its life activity*. Man makes his life activity itself the object of his will and of his consciousness. He has conscious life activity. It is not a determination with which he directly merges. Conscious life activity distinguishes man immediately from animal life activity. It is just because of this that he is a species-being. Or it is only because he is a species-being that he is a conscious being, i.e., that his own life is an object for him. Only because of that is his activity free activity. Estranged labour reverses this relationship, so that it is just because man is a conscious being that he makes his life activity, his *essential being*, a mere means to his *existence*.

In creating a *world of objects* by his practical activity, in his *work upon* inorganic nature, man proves himself a conscious species-being (i.e., as a being that treats the species as its own essential being, or that treats itself as a species-being. Admittedly animals also produce. They build themselves nests, dwellings, like the bees, beavers, ants, etc. But an animal only produces what it immediately needs for itself or its young. It produces one-sidedly, whilst man produces universally. It produces only under the dominion of immediate physical need, whilst man produces even when he is free from physical need and only truly produces in freedom therefrom. An animal produces only itself, whilst man reproduces the whole of nature. An animal's product belongs immediately to its physical body, whilst man freely confronts his product. An animal forms objects only in accordance with the standard and the need of the species to which it belongs, whilst man knows how to produce in accordance with the standard of every species, and knows how to apply everywhere the inherent standard to the object. Man therefore also forms objects in accordance with the laws of beauty.

It is just in his work upon the objective world, therefore, that man really proves himself to be a *species-being*. This production is his active species-life. Through this production, nature appears as *his* work and his reality. The object of labour is, therefore, the *objectification of man's species-life*; for he duplicates himself not only, as in consciousness, intellectually, but also actively, in reality, and therefore he sees himself in a world that he has created. In tearing away from man the object of his production, therefore, estranged labour tears from him his *species-life*, his real objectivity as a member of the species, and transforms his advantage over animals into the disadvantage that his inorganic body, nature, is taken away from him.

Similarly, in degrading spontaneous, free activity to a means, estranged labour makes man's species-life a means to his physical existence.

The consciousness which man has of his species is thus transformed by estrangement in such a way that species [-life] becomes for him a means.

Estranged labour turns thus:

(3) *Man's species-being*, both nature and his spiritual species-property, into a being *alien* to him, into a *means* for his *individual existence*. It estranges from man his own body, as well as external nature and his spiritual aspect, his *human* aspect.

(4) An immediate consequence of the fact that man is estranged from the product of his labour, from his life activity, from his species-being is the *estrangement of man* from *man*. When man confronts himself, he confronts the *other* man. What applies to a man's relation to his work, to the product of his labour and to himself, also holds of a man's relation to the other man, and to the other man's labour and object of labour.

In fact, the proposition that man's species-nature is estranged from him means that one man is estranged from the other, as each of them is from man's essential nature.

The estrangement of man, and in fact every relationship in which man [stands] to himself, is realised and expressed only in the relationship in which a man stands to other men.

Hence within the relationship of estranged labour each man views the other in accordance with the standard and the relationship in which he finds himself as a worker.

[XXV] We took our departure from a fact of political economy – the estrangement of the worker and his product. We have formulated this fact in conceptual terms as *estranged, alienated* labour. We have analysed this concept – hence analysing merely a fact of political economy.

Let us now see, further, how the concept of estranged, alienated labour must express and present itself in real life.

If the product of labour is alien to me, if it confronts me as an alien power, to whom, then, does it belong?

If my own activity does not belong to me, if it is an alien, a coerced activity, to whom, then, does it belong?

To a being *other* than myself.

Who is this being?

The *gods*? To be sure, in the earliest times the principal production (for example, the building of temples, etc., in Egypt, India and Mexico) appears to be in the service of the gods, and the product belongs to the gods. However, the gods on their own were never the lords of labour. No more was *nature*. And what a contradiction it would be if, the more man subjugated nature by his labour and the more the miracles of the gods were rendered superfluous by the miracles of industry, the more man were to renounce the joy of production and the enjoyment of the product to please these powers.

The *alien* being, to whom labour and the product of labour belongs, in whose service labour is done and for whose benefit the product of labour is provided, can only be *man* himself.

If the product of labour does not belong to the worker, if it confronts him as an alien power, then this can only be because it belongs to some *other man than the worker*. If the worker's activity is a torment to him, to another it must give *satisfaction* and pleasure. Not the gods, not nature, but only man himself can be this alien power over man.

We must bear in mind the previous proposition that man's relation to himself only becomes for him *objective* and *actual* through his relation to the other man. Thus, if the product of his labour, his labour objectified, is for him an *alien, hostile*, powerful object independent of him, then his position towards it is such that someone else is master of this object, someone who is alien, hostile, powerful, and independent of him. If he treats his own activity as an unfree activity, then he treats it as an activity performed in the service, under the dominion, the coercion, and the yoke of another man.

Every self-estrangement of man, from himself and from nature, appears in the relation in which he places himself and nature to men other than and differentiated from himself. For this reason religious self-estrangement necessarily appears in the relationship of the layman to the priest, or again to a mediator, etc., since we are here dealing with the intellectual world. In the real practical world self-estrangement can only become manifest through the real practical relationship to other men. The medium through which estrangement takes place is itself *practical*. Thus through estranged labour man not only creates his relationship to the object and to the act of production as to powers that are alien and hostile to him; he also creates the relationship in which other men stand to his production and to his product, and the relationship in which he stands to these other men. Just as he creates his own production as the loss of his reality, as his punishment; his own product as a loss, as a product not belonging to him; so he creates the domination of the person who does not produce over production and over the product. Just as he estranges his own activity from himself, so he confers upon the stranger an activity which is not his own.

We have until now considered this relationship only from the standpoint of the worker and later we shall be considering it also from the standpoint of the non-worker.

Through *estranged, alienated labour*, then, the worker produces the relationship to this labour of a man alien to labour and standing outside it. The relationship of the worker to labour creates the relation to it of the capitalist (or whatever one chooses to call the master of labour). *Private property* is thus the product, the result, the necessary consequence, of *alienated labour*, of the external relation of the worker to nature and to himself.

Private property thus results by analysis from the concept of *alienated labour*, i.e., of *alienated man*, of estranged labour, of estranged life, of *estranged* man.

True, it is as a result of the *movement of private property* that we have obtained the concept of *alienated labour (of alienated life)* in political economy. But analysis of this concept shows that though private property appears to be the reason, the cause of alienated labour, it is rather its consequence, just as the gods are *originally* not the cause but the effect of man's intellectual confusion. Later this relationship becomes reciprocal.

Only at the culmination of the development of private property does this, its secret, appear again, namely, that on the one hand it is the *product* of alienated labour, and that on the other it is the *means* by which labour alienates itself, the *realisation of this alienation*.

This exposition immediately sheds light on various hitherto unsolved conflicts.

(1) Political economy starts from labour as the real soul of production; yet to labour it gives nothing, and to private property everything. Confronting this contradiction, Proudhon has decided in favour of labour against private property. We understand, however, that this apparent contradiction is the contradiction of *estranged labour* with itself, and that political economy has merely formulated the laws of estranged labour.

We also understand, therefore, that *wages* and *private property* are identical. Indeed, where the product, as the object of labour, pays for labour itself, there the wage is but a necessary consequence of labour's estrangement. Likewise, in the wage of labour, labour does not appear as an end in itself but as the servant of the wage. We shall develop this point later, and meanwhile will only draw some conclusions.

[XXVI] An enforced *increase of wages* (disregarding all other difficulties, including the fact that it would only be by force, too, that such an increase, being an anomaly, could be maintained) would therefore be nothing but better *payment for the slave*, and would not win either for the worker or for labour their human status and dignity.

Indeed, even the *equality of wages*, as demanded by Proudhon, only transforms the relationship of the present-day worker to his labour into the relationship of all men to labour. Society is then conceived as an abstract capitalist.

Wages are a direct consequence of estranged labour, and estranged labour is the direct cause of private property. The downfall of the one must therefore involve the downfall of the other.

(2) From the relationship of estranged labour to private property it follows further that the emancipation of society from private property,

etc., from servitude, is expressed in the *political* form of the *emancipation of the workers*; not that *their* emancipation alone is at stake, but because the emancipation of the workers contains universal human emancipation – and it contains this, because the whole of human servitude is involved in the relation of the worker to production, and all relations of servitude are but modifications and consequences of this relation.

Just as we have derived the concept of *private property* from the concept of *estranged, alienated labour* by *analysis*, so we can develop every *category* of political economy with the help of these two factors; and we shall find again in each category, e.g., trade, competition, capital, money, only a *particular* and *developed expression* of these first elements.

Before considering this phenomenon, however, let us try to solve two other problems.

(1) To define the general *nature of private property*, as it has arisen as a result of estranged labour, in its relation to *truly human* and *social property*.

(2) We have accepted the *estrangement of labour*, its *alienation*, as a fact, and we have analysed this fact. How, we now ask, does *man* come to *alienate*, to estrange, his *labour*? How is this estrangement rooted in the nature of human development? We have already gone a long way to the solution of this problem by *transforming* the question of the *origin of private property* into the question of the relation of *alienated labour* to the course of humanity's development. For when one speaks of *private property*, one thinks of dealing with something external to man. When one speaks of labour, one is directly dealing with man himself. This new formulation of the question already contains its solution.

As to (1): The general nature of private property and its relation to truly human property.

Alienated labour has resolved itself for us into two components which depend on one another, or which are but different expressions of one and the same relationship. *Appropriation* appears as *estrangement, as alienation*; and *alienation* appears as *appropriation, estrangement* as truly *becoming a citizen*.

We have considered the one side – *alienated* labour in relation to the worker himself, i.e., the *relation of alienated labour to itself*. The product, the necessary outcome of this relationship, as we have seen, is the *property relation of the non-worker to the worker and to labour*. *Private property*, as the material, summary expression of alienated labour, embraces both relations – the *relation of the worker to labour and to the product of his labour and to the non-worker*, and the relation of the *non-worker to the worker and to the product of his labour*.

Having seen that in relation to the worker who *appropriates* nature by means of his labour, this appropriation appears as estrangement, his own spontaneous activity as activity for another and as activity of another, vitality as a sacrifice of life, production of the object at loss of the object to an alien power, to an *alien* person – we shall now consider the relation to the worker, to labour and its object of this person who is *alien* to labour and the worker.

First it has to be noted that everything which appears in the worker as an *activity of alienation, of estrangement*, appears in the non-worker as a *state of alienation, of estrangement*.

Secondly, that the worker's *real, practical attitude* in production and to the product (as a state of mind) appears in the non-worker confronting him as a *theoretical* attitude.

[XXVII] *Thirdly*, the non-worker does everything against the worker which the worker does against himself; but he does not do against himself what he does against the worker.

Let us look more closely at these three relations.[1]

NOTE
1. At this point the first manuscript breaks off unfinished. [*Ed.*]

14

[THE POWER OF MONEY]

[XLI] If man's *feelings*, passions, etc., are not merely anthropological phenomena in the [narrower] sense, but truly *ontological* affirmations of being (of nature), and if they are only really affirmed because their *object* exists for them as a *sensual* object, then it is clear that:

(1) They have by no means merely one mode in affirmation, but rather that the distinct character of their existence, of their life, is constituted by the distinct mode of their affirmation. In what manner the object exists for them, is the characteristic mode of their *gratification*.

(2) Wherever the sensuous affirmation is the direct annulment of the object in its independent form (as in eating, drinking, working up of the object, etc.), this is the affirmation of the object.

(3) Insofar as man, and hence also his feeling, etc., is *human*, the affirmation of the object by another is likewise his own gratification.

(4) Only through developed industry – i.e., through the medium of private property – does the ontological essence of human passion come into being, in its totality as well as in its humanity; the science of man is therefore itself a product of man's own practical activity.

(5) The meaning of private property – apart from its estrangement – is the *existence of essential objects* for man, both as objects of enjoyment and as objects of activity.

By possessing the *property* of buying everything, by possessing the property of appropriating all objects, *money* is thus the *object* of eminent possession. The universality of its *property* is the omnipotence of its being. It is therefore regarded as omnipotent ... Money is the *procurer* between man's need and the object, between his life and his means of life. But *that which* mediates *my* life for me, also *mediates* the existence of other people for me. For me it is the *other* person.

> What, man! Confound it, hands and feet
> And head and backside, all are yours!
> And what we take while life is sweet,
> Is that to be declared not ours?

> Six stallions, say, I can afford,
> Is not their strength my property?
> I tear along, a sporting lord,
> As if their legs belonged to me.

Goethe: Faust(Mephistopheles)[1]

Shakespeare in *Timon of Athens*:

> Gold? Yellow, glittering, precious gold? No, Gods,
> I am no idle votarist! ...
> Thus much of this will make black white, foul fair,
> Wrong right, base noble, old young, coward valiant.
> ... Why, this
> Will lug your priests and servants from your sides,
> Pluck stout men's pillows from below their heads:
> This yellow slave
> Will knit and break religions, bless the accursed;
> Make the hoar leprosy adored, place thieves
> And give them title, knee and approbation
> With senators on the bench: This is it
> That makes the wappen'd widow wed again;
> She, whom the spital-house and ulcerous sores
> Would cast the gorge at, this embalms and spices
> To the April day again. Come, damned earth,

Thou common whore of mankind, that put'st odds
Among the rout of nations.

And also later:

'O thou sweet king-killer, and dear divorce
'Twixt natural son and sire! Thou bright defiler
Of Hymen's purest bed! Thou valiant Mars!
Thou ever young, fresh, loved and delicate wooer,
Whose blush doth thaw the consecrated snow
That lies on Dian's lap! Thou *visible God*!
That solder'st *close impossibilities*,
And makest them kiss! That speak'st with every tongue,
[XLII] To every purpose! O thou touch of hearts!
Think, thy slave man rebels, and by thy virtue
Set them into confounding odds, that beasts
May have the world in empire![2]

Shakespeare excellently depicts the real nature of *money*. To understand him, let us begin, first of all, by expounding the passage from Goethe.

That which is for me through the medium of *money* – that for which I can pay (i.e., which money can buy) – that am I *myself*, the possessor of the money. The extent of the power of money is the extent of my power. Money's properties are my – the possessor's – properties and essential powers. Thus, what I *am* and *am capable of* is by no means determined by my individuality. I *am* ugly, but I can buy for myself the *most beautiful* of women. Therefore I am not *ugly*, for the effect of *ugliness*- its deterrent power – is nullified by money. I, according to my individual characteristics, am *lame*, but money furnishes me with twenty-four feet. Therefore I am not lame. I am bad, dishonest, unscrupulous, stupid; but money is honoured, and hence its possessor. Money is the supreme good, therefore its possessor is good. Money, besides, saves me the trouble of being dishonest: I am therefore presumed honest. I am *brainless*, but money is the *real brain* of all things and how then should its possessor be brainless? Besides, he can buy clever people for himself, and is he who has power over the clever not more clever than the clever? Do not I, who thanks to money am capable of *all* that the human heart longs for, possess all human capacities? Does not my money, therefore, transform all my incapacities into their contrary?

If *money* is the bond binding me to *human* life, binding society to me, connecting me with nature and man, is not money the bond of all *bonds*? Can it not dissolve and bind all ties? Is it not, therefore, also the universal *agent of separation*? It is the *coin* that really *separates* as well as the real *binding agent*- the [...] *chemical* power of society.

Shakespeare stresses especially two properties of money:

(1) It is the visible divinity – the transformation of all human and natural properties into their contraries, the universal confounding and distorting of things: impossibilities are soldered together by it.
(2) It is the common whore, the common procurer of people and nations.

The distorting and confounding of all human and natural qualities, the fraternisation of impossibilities – the *divine* power of money – lies in its *character* as men's estranged, alienating and self-disposing *species-nature*. Money is the alienated *ability of mankind*.

That which I am unable to do as a *man*, and of which therefore all my individual essential powers are incapable, I am able to do by means of *money*. Money thus turns each of these powers into something which in itself is not – turns it, that is, into its *contrary*

If I long for a particular dish or want to take the mail-coach because I am not strong enough to go by foot, money fetches me the dish and the mail-coach: that is, it converts my wishes from something in the realm of imagination, translates them from their meditated, imagined or desired existence into their *sensuous, actual* existence – from imagination to life, from imagined being into real being. In effecting this mediation, [money] is the *truly creative* power.

No doubt the *demand* also exists for him who has no money, but his demand is a mere thing of the imagination without effect or existence for me, for a third party, for the [others], [XLIII] and which therefore remains even for me *unreal* and *objectless*. The difference between effective demand based on money and ineffective demand based on my need, my passion, my wish, etc., is the difference between *being* and *thinking*, between the idea which merely *exists* within me and the idea which exists as a *real object* outside of me.

If I have no money for travel, I have no *need* – that is, no real and realisable need – to travel. If I have the *vocation* for study but no money for it, I have *no* vocation for study – that is, no *effective*, no *true* vocation. On the other hand, if I have really *no* vocation for study but have the will *and* the money for it, I have an *effective* vocation for it. *Money* as the external, universal *medium* and *faculty* (not springing from man as man or from human society as society) for turning an *image into reality and reality into a mere image*, transforms the *real essential powers of man and nature* into what are merely abstract notions and therefore *imperfections* and tormenting chimeras, just as it transforms *real imperfections and chimeras-* essential powers which are really impotent, which exist only in the imagination of the individual – into *real essential powers* and *faculties*. In the light of this characteristic alone, money is thus the general distorting of *individualities* which turns them into their opposite and confers contradictory attributes upon their attributes.

Money, then, appears as this *distorting* power both against the individual and against the bonds of society, etc., which claim to be *entities* in themselves. It transforms fidelity into infidelity, love into hate, hate into love, virtue into vice, vice into virtue, servant into master, master into servant, idiocy into intelligence, and intelligence into idiocy.

Since money, as the existing and active concept of value, confounds and confuses all things, it is the general *confounding* and *confusing* of all things – the world upside-down – the confounding and confusing of all natural and human qualities.

He who can buy bravery is brave, though he be a coward. As money is not exchanged for any one specific quality, for any one specific thing, or for any particular human essential power, but for the entire objective world of man and nature, from the standpoint of its possessor it therefore serves to exchange every quality for every other, even contradictory, quality and object: it is the fraternisation of impossibilities. It makes contradictions embrace.

Assume *man* to be *man* and his relationship to the world to be a human one: then you can exchange love only for love, trust for trust, etc. If you want to enjoy art, you must be an artistically cultivated person; if you want to exercise influence over other people, you must be a person with a stimulating and encouraging effect on other people. Every one of your relations to men and to nature must be a *specific expression*, corresponding to the object of your will, of your *real individual* life. If you love without evoking love in return – that is, if your loving as loving does not produce reciprocal love; if through a *living expression* of yourself as a loving person you do not make yourself a *beloved one*, then your love is impotent – a misfortune. [XLIII]

NOTES

1. Goethe, *Faust*, Part 1, Faust's Study; the English translation is taken from Goethe's *Faust*, Part 1, translated by Philip Wayne, Penguin, 1949, p91. [*Ed.*]
2. Shakespeare, *Timon of Athens*, Act IV, Scene 3. (Marx quotes the Schlegel-Tieck translation.). [*Ed.*]

15

BREAD MANUFACTURE

Garibaldi, the American Civil War, the revolution in Greece, the cotton crisis, Veillard's bankruptcy – everything is overshadowed for the moment in London by the – *question of bread*, but the question of bread in the literal sense. The English, who are so proud of their 'ideas in iron and steam', have suddenly discovered that they have been making the 'staff of life' in the same antediluvian manner as at the time of the Norman Conquest. The only essential progress consists in the adulteration of the foodstuffs that modern chemistry has facilitated. It is an old British proverb that every man, even the best, must eat 'a peck of dirt' in his lifetime. This was meant in the moral sense. John Bull has not the slightest suspicion that he is eating, in the coarsest physical sense, an incredible *mixtum compositum*[1] of flour, alum, cobwebs, black beetles, and human sweat. Being the bible reader he is, he knew, of course, that man earns his bread in the sweat of his brow;[2] but it was something brand-new to him that human sweat must enter into bread dough as a seasoning.

The sequence of steps in which big industry appropriates the various territories in which it finds handiwork, artisanship and manufacture established seems preposterous at first sight. Producing wheat, for example, is a rural occupation, and baking bread an urban one. Should it not be expected that industrial production would take over the urban trade earlier than the rural one? And yet things have gone in the opposite direction. Wherever we look, we shall find that the most immediate needs have thus far avoided the influence of large-scale industry, with more or less obstinacy, and their satisfaction depends upon the hopelessly detailed craft methods of ancient tradition. It is not England but North America that first made a breach in this tradition, and that only in our times. The Yankee was the first to apply machinery to tailoring, bootmaking, etc., and even transferred them from the factory into the private house. The phenomenon can easily be explained, however. Industrial production calls for mass production, on a large scale, for commerce, instead of for private consumption, and by the nature of things raw materials and semi-manufactured goods are the *first* things it takes over, and finished goods destined for immediate consumption the *last*.

Now, however, the hour of the downfall of the *master* bakers and of the rise of the bread *manufacturer* seems to have struck in England. The disgust and loathing evoked by Mr *Tremenheere*'s disclosures as to the 'mysteries of bread'[3] would not by themselves have been sufficient to produce such a revolution if it were not for the added circumstance that capital, in large amounts driven by the American crisis out of domains it has long monopolised, is anxiously looking for new fields to settle down in.

The journeymen at the London bakeries had flooded Parliament with petitions protesting their exceptionally wretched condition. The Home Secretary[4] appointed Mr Tremenheere investigator and a kind of examining magistrate into these complaints. Mr Tremenheere's report is divided into two main sections. The first describes the wretched state of the workers in the bakeries; the second reveals the disgusting mysteries of breadmaking itself.

The first part portrays the journeymen in the bakeries as 'the white slaves of civilisation'. Their usual working hours begin at 11 in the evening and last until 3 or 4 in the afternoon. The work increases towards the weekend. In most London bakeries it continues without a break from 10 o'clock Thursday evening till Saturday night. The average life-span of these workers, most of whom die of consumption, is 42 years.

As for the breadmaking itself, it takes place for the most part in cramped underground vaults either ventilated badly or not at all. In addition to lack of ventilation, there are the pestilential vapours from bad outlet ducts, 'and the fermenting bread gets impregnated with the noxious gases surrounding it'. Cobwebs, black beetles, rats and mice are 'incorporated with the dough'.

> 'It was with the utmost reluctance,' says Mr Tremenheere, 'that I came to the conclusion that a batch of dough is rarely made without having more or less of the perspiration, and often of the more morbid secretions, of the men who make it mixed up with it.'

Even the finest bakeries are not free from these revolting abominations, but they reach an indescribably low point in the holes where the bread of the poor is baked, and where too the adulteration of the flour with alum and bone-earth is practised most freely.

Mr Tremenheere proposes stricter laws against adulteration of bread, as well as putting the bakeries under government supervision, limiting the working hours for 'young people' (i.e., those who have not reached the age of 18) from 5 in the morning to 9 at night, and so forth, but very reasonably does not expect the elimination of the abuses, which arise out of the old method of production itself, to come from Parliament, but from large-scale industry.

As a matter of fact, the *Stevens* machine for preparing dough has already been installed in certain places. There is another, similar machine at the industrial exhibition. Both still leave too much of the baking process to manual work. On the other hand, Dr *Dauglish* has revolutionised the entire process of making bread. From the moment the flour leaves the hopper to the time the bread goes into the oven, no human hand touches it in this system. Dr Dauglish does away with yeast entirely and effects fermentation by the use of carbonic acid. He reduces the entire operation of making bread, including the baking, from eight hours to 30 minutes. Night work is entirely done away with. The employment of carbonic acid gas interdicts any admixture of adulterants. A great saving is made by the changed method of fermentation, and also in particular by combining the new machinery with an American invention, by which the gritty coating of the grain is removed without, as previously, destroying three-fourths of the bran, which is the most nutritious part of the grain, according to the French chemist, Mége Mouriès, Dr Dauglish calculates that his process would save England 8 million pounds sterling in flour every year. Another saving is in coal consumption. The cost of coal, including the steam engine, for the oven, is reduced from 1 shilling to 3 pence. The carbonic acid gas, prepared from the best sulfuric acid, costs about 9 pence per sack, while at the present time the yeast comes to over a shilling for the bakers.

A bakery on the now much improved method of Dr Dauglish was installed some time ago in a part of London, at Dockhead, Bermondsey, but went out of business because of the unfavourable location of the shop. At the present time, similar plants are operating in Portsmouth, Dublin, Leeds, Bath, and Coventry, and, it is said, with very satisfying results. The plant recently installed in Islington (a suburb of London) under Dr Dauglish's personal supervision is aimed more at training the workers than at sales. Preparations for introducing the machinery on a large scale are being made at the municipal bakery of Paris.

General adoption of the Dauglish method will turn most of today's English master bakers into mere agents of a few large bread manufacturers. They will only be engaged in retail selling thereafter, not with production; and for most of them that will not be a particularly painful metamorphosis, since in point of fact they are already only agents of the large millers. The triumph of machine-made bread will mark a turning point in the history of large-scale industry, the point at which it will storm the hitherto doggedly defended last ditch of medieval artisanship.

Written on October 26, 1862
First published in *Die Presse*, No 299, October 30, 1862
Printed according to the newspaper

NOTES
1. Hodge-podge. [*Ed.*]
2. *Genesis*, 3:19. [*Ed.*]

3. This refers to the *Report Addressed to Her Majesty's Principal Secretary of State for the Home Department, Relative to the Grievances Complained of by the Journeymen Bakers*, London, 1862. [*Ed.*]
4. G. Grey. [*Ed.*]

Section 7: Capital, money, wages and trade

Marx believed that the value of goods was established in general relation to the amount of labour spent in their production. This labour theory of value has come in for enormous criticism over the past few years, in almost every area of economic teaching – but not in globalisation theory, where an unlikely variant of the same argument is used. If the cost of labour determines the price of a commodity, then surely it follows that production must move to that area where labour is cheapest? A similar case was put in Marx's time, and he was duly sceptical. The extracts here show Marx's attempts to make sense of world trade, the price of commodities, and the relationships out of which goods could be exchanged.

The first extract in this section is taken from *Value, Price and Profit* (the pamphlet has also been published as 'Wages, Price and Profit'), an address given to the General Council of the International Working Men's Association in June 1865. The membership of the Council came from two distinct groups, socialist refugees from Europe and British trade unionists. This latter group were concerned by the teachings of

John Weston, a follower of Robert Owen, who maintained that trade union action must be counter-productive – in that it would force up the price of goods, harming the workers concerned. Although Weston was a socialist, the argument itself was little different from the theories of today. In this passage, Marx showed that many different factors could determine the price of any specific commodity. The notion that workers should decline to organise could only harm the workers themselves: 'If [the labourer] resigned himself to accept the will, the dictates of the capitalist as a permanent economical law, he would share in the miseries of the slave, without the security of the slave'.

The second extract tackles directly the notion that manufacture will necessarily move to those regions where labour is worst paid. Here Marx addresses the value of goods and currency in different regions. Where labour is less productive workers will receive less pay. But the price of goods will also be less, meaning that the unit of capital is less efficient and less profits are made. Ask any employer whether they would rather establish their company in a wealthy region with the advantages of a market, skilled workers and cheap transport – or in a poorer region without those benefits – and you will see Marx's point.

The third passage in this section addresses the claim that the storing of produced goods could be kept to a minimum. This is one of the theories behind 'just-in-time' or 'flexible' working – that labour should be taken on only after an item has been purchased. Thus even the employment of labour could be subordinated to the sale of commodities. Writing in the 1860s, Marx wondered aloud whether such a system could even be possible. His suggestion was that flexibility in warehousing could only be achieved if companies were absolutely inflexible in their choice of raw materials. Capitalists may have desired the absolute subordination of labour, but such a triumph could never be achieved.

16

MAIN CASES OF ATTEMPTS AT RAISING WAGES OR RESISTING THEIR FALL

Let us now seriously consider the main cases in which a rise of wages is attempted or a reduction of wages resisted.

1. We have seen that the *value of the labouring power*, or in more popular parlance, the *value of labour*, is determined by the value of necessaries, or the quantity of labour required to produce them. If, then, in a given country the value of the daily average necessaries of the labourer represented six hours of labour expressed in three shillings, the labourer would have to work six hours daily to produce an equivalent for his daily maintenance. If the whole working day was twelve hours, the capitalist would pay him the value of his labour by paying him three shillings. Half the working day would be unpaid labour, and the rate of profit would amount to 100 per cent. But now suppose that, consequent upon a decrease of productivity, more labour should be wanted to produce, say, the same amount of agricultural produce, so that the price of the average daily necessaries should rise from three to four shillings. In that case the *value* of labour would rise by one-third, or 33⅓ per cent. Eight hours of the working day would be required to produce an equivalent for the daily maintenance of the labourer, according to his old standard of living. The surplus-labour would therefore sink from six hours to four, and the rate of profit from 100 to 50 per cent. But in insisting upon a rise of wages, the labourer would only insist upon getting the *increased value of his labour*, like every other seller of a commodity, who, the costs of his commodities having increased, tries to get its increased value paid. If wages did not rise, or not sufficiently rise, to compensate for the increased values of necessaries, the *price* of labour

would sink *below the value of labour*, and the labourer's standard of life would deteriorate.

But a change might also take place in an opposite direction. By virtue of the increased productivity of labour, the same amount of the average daily necessaries might sink from three to two shillings, or only four hours out of the working day, instead of six, be wanted to reproduce an equivalent for the value of the daily necessaries. The working man would now be able to buy with two shillings as many necessaries as he did before with three shillings. Indeed, the *value of labour* would have sunk, but that diminished value would command the same amount of commodities as before. Then profits would rise from three to four shillings, and, the rate of profit from 100 to 200 per cent. Although the labourer's absolute standard of life would have remained the same, his *relative* wages, and therewith his *relative social position*, as compared with that of the capitalist, would have been lowered. If the working man should resist that reduction of relative wages, he would only try to get some share in the increased productive powers of his own labour, and to maintain his former relative position in the social scale. Thus, after the abolition of the Corn Laws, and in flagrant violation of the most solemn pledges given during the anti-corn law agitation, the English factory lords generally reduced wages ten per cent. The resistance of the workmen was at first baffled, but, consequent upon circumstances I cannot now enter upon, the ten per cent. lost were afterwards regained.

2. The *values* of necessaries, and consequently the *value of labour*, might remain the same, but a change might occur in their *money prices*, consequent upon a previous *change* in the *value of money*.

By the discovery of more fertile mines and so forth, two ounces of gold might, for example, cost no more labour to produce than one ounce did before. The *value* of gold would then be depreciated by one half, or fifty per cent. As the *values* of all other commodities would then be expressed in twice their former *money prices*, so also the same with the *value of labour*. Twelve hours of labour, formerly expressed in six shillings, would now be expressed in twelve shillings. If the working man's wages should remain three shillings, instead of rising to six shillings, the *money price of his labour* would only be equal to *half the value of his labour*, and his standard of life would fearfully deteriorate. This would also happen in a greater or lesser degree if his wages should rise, but not proportionately to the fall in the value of gold. In such a case nothing would have been changed, either in the productive powers of labour, or in supply and demand, or in values. Nothing could have changed except the money *names* of those values. To say that in such a case the workman ought not to insist upon a proportionate rise of wages, is to say that he must be content to be paid with names, instead of with things. All past history proves that whenever such a depreciation of money occurs the capitalists are on the alert to seize this opportunity for defrauding the workman. A very large school of political economists assert that, consequent upon the new discoveries of gold lands, the better working of silver mines, and the cheaper supply of quicksilver, the value of precious metals has been again depreciated. This would explain the general and simultaneous attempts on the Continent at a rise of wages.

3. We have till now supposed that the *working day* has given limits. The working day, however, has, by itself, no constant limits. It is the constant tendency of capital to stretch it to its utmost physically possibly length, because in the same degree surplus-labour, and consequently the profit resulting therefrom, will be increased. The more capital succeeds in prolonging the working day, the greater the amount of other people's labour it will appropriate. During the seventeenth and even the first two-thirds of the eighteenth century a ten hours' working day was the normal working day all over England. During the anti-Jacobin war, which was in fact a war waged by the British barons against the British working masses capital celebrated its bacchanalia, and prolonged the working day from ten to twelve, fourteen, eighteen hours. *Malthus*, by no means a man whom you would suspect of a maudlin sentimentalism, declared in a pamphlet, published about 1815, that if this sort of things was to go on the life of the nation would be attacked at its very source. A few years before the general introduction of the newly-invented machinery about 1765, a pamphlet appeared in England under the title, *An Essay on Trade*. The anony-

mous author, an avowed enemy of the working classes, declaims on the necessity of expanding the limits of the working day. Amongst other means to this end, he proposes *working houses*, which, he says, ought to be *"Houses of Terror"*. And what is the length of the working day he prescribes for these *"Houses of Terror"*? *Twelve hours*, the very same time which in 1832 was declared by capitalists, political economists, and ministers to be not only the existing but the necessary time of labour for a child under twelve years.

By selling his labouring power, and he must do so under the present system, the working man makes over to the capitalist the consumption of that power, but within certain rational limits. He sells his labouring power in order to maintain it, apart from its natural wear and tear, but not to destroy it. In selling his labouring power at its daily or weekly value, it is understood that in one day or one week that labouring power shall not be submitted to two days' or two weeks' waste or wear and tear. Take a machine worth £1,000. If it is used up in ten years it will add to the value of the commodities in whose production it assists £100 yearly. If it be used up in five years it would add £200 yearly, or the value of its annual wear and tear is in inverse ratio to the quickness with which it is consumed. But this distinguishes the working man from the machine. Machinery does not wear out exactly in the same ratio in which it is used. Man, on the contrary, decays in a greater ratio than would be visible from the mere numerical addition of work

In their attempts at reducing the working day to its former rational dimensions, or, where they cannot enforce a legal fixation of a normal working day, at checking overwork by a rise of wages, a rise not only in proportion to the surplus-time exacted, but in a greater proportion, working men fulfil only a duty to themselves and their race. They only set limits to the tyrannical usurpations of capital. Time is the room of human development. A man who has no free time to dispose of, whose whole lifetime, apart from the mere physical interruptions by sleep, meals, and so forth, is absorbed by his labour for the capitalist, is less than a beast of burden. He is a mere machine for producing Foreign Wealth, broken in body and brutalised in mind. Yet the whole history of modern industry shows that capital, if not checked, will recklessly and ruthlessly work to cast down the whole working class to the utmost state of degradation.

In prolonging the working day the capitalist may pay *higher wages* and still lower the *value of labour*, if the rise of wages does not correspond to the greater amount of labour extracted, and the quicker decay of the labouring power thus caused. This may be done in another way. Your middle-class statisticians will tell you, for instance, that the average wages of factory families in Lancashire have risen. They forget that instead of the labour of the man, the head of the family, his wife and perhaps three or four children are now thrown under the Juggernaut wheels of capital, and that the rise of the aggregate wages does not correspond to the aggregate surplus-labour extracted from the family.

Even with given limits of the working day, such as now exist in all branches of industry subjected to the factory laws, a rise of wages may become necessary', if only to keep up the old standard *value of labour*. By increasing the *intensity* of labour, a man may be made to expend as much vital force in one hour as he formerly did in two. This has, to a certain degree, been effected in the trades, placed under the Factory Acts, by the acceleration of machinery, and the greater number of working machines which a single individual has now to superintend. If the increase in the intensity of labour or the mass of labour spent in an hour keeps some fair proportion to the decrease in the extent of the working day, the working man will still be the winner. If this limit is overshot, he loses in one form what he has gained in another, and ten hours of labour may then become as ruinous as twelve hours were before. In checking this tendency of capital, by struggling for a rise of wages corresponding to the rising intensity of labour, the working man only resists the depreciation of his labour and the deterioration of his race.

4. All of you know that, from reasons I have not now to explain, capitalistic production moves through certain periodical cycles. It moves through a state of quiescence, growing animation, prosperity, overtrade, crisis, and stagnation. The market prices of commodities, and the market rates of profit, follow these phases, now sinking below their averages, now rising above them. Considering the whole cycle, you will find that one deviation of the market price is being compen-

sated by the other, and that, taking the average of the cycle, the market prices of commodities are regulated by their values. Well! During the phase of sinking market prices and the phases of crisis and stagnation, the working man, if not thrown out of employment altogether, is sure to have his wages lowered. Not to be defrauded, he must, even with such a fall of market prices, debate with the capitalist in what proportional degree a fall of wages has become necessary. If, during the phases of prosperity, when extra profits are made, he did not battle for a rise of wages, he would, taking the average of one industrial cycle, not even receive his *average wages*, or the *value* of his labour. It is the utmost height of folly to demand that while his wages are necessarily affected by the adverse phases of the cycle, he should exclude himself from compensation during the prosperous phases of the cycle. Generally, the *values* of all commodities are only realised by the compensation of the continuously changing market prices, springing from the continuous fluctuations of demand and supply. On the basis of the present system labour is only a commodity like others. It must, therefore, pass through the same fluctuations to fetch an average price corresponding to its value. It would be absurd to treat it on the one hand as a commodity, and to want on the other hand to exempt it from the laws which regulate the prices of commodities. The slave receives a permanent and fixed amount of maintenance; the wages labourer does not. He must try to get a rise of wages in the one instance, if only to compensate for a fall of wages in the other. If he resigned himself to accept the will, the dictates of the capitalist as a permanent economical law, he would share in all the miseries of the slave, without the security of the slave.

5. In all the cases I have considered, and they form ninety-nine out of a hundred, you have seen that a struggle for a rise of wages follows only in the track of *previous* changes, and is the necessary offspring of previous changes in the amount of production, the productive powers of labour, the value of labour, the value of money, the extent or the intensity of labour extracted, the fluctuations of market prices, dependent upon the fluctuations of demand and supply, and consistent with the different phases of the industrial cycle; in one word, as reactions of

labour against the previous action of capital. By treating the struggle for a rise of wages independently of all these circumstances, by looking only upon the change of wages, and overlooking all the other changes from which they emanate, you proceed from a false premise in order to arrive at false conclusions.

17

NATIONAL DIFFERENCES OF WAGES

In the 17th chapter we were occupied with the manifold combinations which may bring about a change in magnitude of the value of labour-power – this magnitude being considered either absolutely or relatively, i.e., as compared with surplus-value; whilst on the other hand, the quantum of the means of subsistence in which the price of labour is realised might again undergo fluctuations independent of, or different from, the changes of this price.[1] As has been already said, the simple translation of the value, or respectively of the price, of labour-power into the exoteric form of wages transforms all these laws into laws of the fluctuations of wages. That which appears in these fluctuations of wages within a single country as a series of varying combinations, may appear in different countries as contemporaneous difference of national wages. In the comparison of the wages in different nations, we must therefore take into account all the factors that determine changes in the amount of the value of labour-power; the price and the extent of the prime necessaries of life as naturally and historically developed, the cost of training the labourers, the part played by the labour of women and children, the productiveness of labour, its extensive and intensive magnitude. Even the most superficial comparison requires the reduction first of the average day-wage for the same trades, in different countries, to a uniform working-day. After this reduction to the same terms of the day-wages, time-wage must again be translated into piece-wage, as the latter only can be a measure both of the productivity and the intensity of labour.

In every country there is a certain average intensity of labour, below which the labour for the production of a commodity requires more than the socially necessary time, and therefore does not reckon as labour of normal quality. Only a degree of intensity above the national average affects, in a given country, the measure of value by the mere duration of the working-time. This is not the case on the universal market, whose integral parts are the individual countries. The average intensity of labour changes from country to country; here it is greater, there less. These national averages form a scale, whose unit of measure is the average unit of universal labour. The more intense national labour, therefore, as compared with the less intense, produces in the same time more value, which expresses itself in more money.

But the law of value in its international application is yet more modified by this, that on the world-market the more productive national labour reckons also as the more intense, so long as the more productive nation is not compelled by competition to lower the selling price of its commodities to the level of their value.

In proportion as capitalist production is developed in a country, in the same proportion do the national intensity and productivity of labour there rise above the international level. The different quantities of commodities of the same kind, produced in different countries in the same working-time, have, therefore, unequal international values, which are expressed in different prices, i.e., in sums of money varying according to international values. The relative value of money will, therefore, be less in the nation with more developed capitalist mode of production than in the nation with less developed. It follows, then, that the nominal wages, the equivalent of labour-power expressed in money, will also be higher in the first nation than in the second; which does not at all prove that this holds also for the real wages, i.e., for the means of subsistence placed at the disposal of the labourer.

But even apart from these relative differences of the value of money in different countries, it will be found, frequently, that the daily or weekly, &c., wage in the first nation is higher than in the second, whilst the relative price of labour, i.e., the price of labour as compared both with surplus-value and with the value of the product, stands higher in the second than in the first.[2]

J.W. Cowell, member of the Factory Commission of 1833, after careful investigation of the spinning trade, came to the conclusion that, 'in England wages are virtually lower to the capitalist, though higher to the operative than on the Continent of Europe'.[3] The English Factory Inspector, Alexander Redgrave, in his Report of Oct. 31st 1866, proves by comparative statistics with Continental states, that in spite of lower wages and much longer working-time, Continental labour is, in proportion to the product, dearer than English. An English manager of a cotton factory in Oldenburg, declares that the working-time there lasted from 5.30 am to 8 pm, Saturdays included, and that the workpeople there, when under English overlookers, did not supply during this time quite so much product as the English in 10 hours, but under German overlookers much less. Wages are much lower than in England, in many cases 50 per cent, but the number of hands in proportion to the machinery was much greater, in certain departments in the proportion of 5:3 – Mr Redgrave gives very full details as to the Russian cotton factories. The data were given him by an English manager until recently employed there. On this Russian soil, so fruitful of all infamies, the old horrors of the early days of English factories are in full swing. The managers are, of course, English, as the native Russian capitalist is of no use in factory business. Despite all over-work, continued day and night, despite the most shameful under-payment of the workpeople, Russian manufacture manages to vegetate only by prohibition of foreign competition. I give, in conclusion, a comparative table of Mr Redgrave's, on the average number of spindles per factory and per spinner in the different countries of Europe. He, himself, remarks that he had collected these figures a few years ago, and that since that time the size of the factories and the number of spindles per labourer in England has increased. He supposes, however, an approximately equal progress in the Continental countries mentioned, so that the numbers given would still have their value for purposes of comparison.

AVERAGE NUMBER OF SPINDLES PER FACTORY

England, average of spindles per factory				12,600
France	''	''	''	1,500
Prussia	''	''	''	1,500
Belgium	''	''	''	4,000
Saxony	''	''	''	4,500
Austria	''	''	''	7,000
Switzerland	''	''	''	8,000

AVERAGE NUMBER OF PERSONS EMPLOYED TO SPINDLES

France	one person	to	14	spindles
Russia	''	''	28	''
Prussia	''	''	37	''
Bavaria	''	''	46	''
Austria	''	''	49	''
Belgium	''	''	50	''
Saxony	''	''	50	''
Switzerland	''	''	55	''
Smaller States of Germany	''	''	55	''
Great Britain	''	''	74	''

'This comparison' says Mr Redgrave, 'is yet more unfavourable to Great Britain, inasmuch as there is so large a number of factories in which weaving by power is carried on in conjunction with spinning [whilst in the table the weavers are not deducted], and the factories abroad are chiefly spinning factories; if it were possible to compare like with like, strictly, I could find many cotton spinning factories in my district in which mules containing 2,200 spindles are minded by one man (the 'minder') and two assistants only, turning off daily 220 lbs. Of yarn, measuring 400 miles in length.' (Reports of Insp. Of Fact., 31st Oct., 1866, pp31-37, passim.)

It is well known that in Eastern Europe as well as in Asia, English companies have undertaken the construction of railways, and have, in making them, employed side by side with the native labourers, a certain number of English working-men. Compelled by practical necessity, they thus have had to take into account the national difference in the intensity of labour, but this has brought them no loss. Their experience shows that even if the height of wages corresponds more or less with the average intensity of labour, the relative price of labour varies generally in the inverse direction.

In an 'Essay on the Rate of Wages',[4] one of his first economic writings, H. Carey tries to prove that the wages in the different nations are directly proportional to the degree of productiveness of the national working-days, in order to draw from this international relation, the conclusion that wages everywhere rise and fall in proportion to the productiveness of labour.

The whole of our analysis of the production of surplus-value shows the absurdity of this conclusion, even if Carey himself had proved his premises, instead of, after his usual uncritical and superficial fashion, shuffling to and fro a confused mass of statistical materials. The best of it is that he does not assert that things actually are as they ought to be according to his theory. For State intervention has falsified the natural economic relations. The different national wages must be reckoned, therefore, as if that part of each that goes to the State in the form of taxes, came to the labourer himself. Ought not Mr Carey to consider further whether those 'State expenses' are not the 'natural' fruits of capitalistic development? The reasoning is quite worthy of the man who first declared the relations of capitalist production to be eternal laws of Nature and reason, whose free, harmonious working is only disturbed by the intervention of the State, in order afterwards to discover that the diabolical influence of England on the world-market (an influence, which, it appears, does not spring from the natural laws of capitalist production) necessitates State intervention, i.e., the protection of those laws of Nature and reason by the State, *alias* the System of Protection. He discovered further, that the theorems of Ricardo and others, in which existing social antagonisms and contradictions are formulated, are not the ideal product of the real economic movement, but on the contrary, that the real antagonisms of capitalist production in England and elsewhere are the result of the theories of Ricardo and others! Finally he discovered that it is, in the last resort, commerce that destroys the inborn beauties and harmonies of the capitalist mode of production. A step further, and he will, perhaps, discover that the one evil in capitalist production is capital itself. Only a man with such atrocious want of the critical faculty and such spurious erudition deserved, in spite of his Protectionist heresy, to become the secret source of the harmonious wisdom of a Bastiat, and of all the other Free-trade optimists of today.

NOTES

1. 'It is not accurate to say that wages' (he deals here with their money expression) 'are increased, because they purchase more of a cheaper article', David Buchanan in *Observations on the Subjects Treated in Dr Smith's 'Inquiry into the Nature and Causes of the Wealth of Nations*, Edinburgh 1814.

2. James Anderson remarks in his polemic against Adam Smith: 'It deserves, likewise, to be remarked, that although the apparent price of labour is usually lower in poor countries, where the produce of the soil, and grain in general, is cheap; yet it is in fact for the most part really higher than in other countries. For it is not the wages that is given to the labourer per day that constitutes the real price of labour, although it is its apparent price. The real price is that which a certain quantity of work performed actually costs the employer; and considered in this light, labour is in almost all cases cheaper in rich countries than in those that are poorer, although the price of grain, and other provisions, is usually much lower in the last than in the first ... Labour estimated by the day, is much lower in Scotland than in England ... Labour by the piece is generally cheaper in England', James Anderson, *Observations on the Means of Exciting a Spirit of National Industry, &c.*, Edinburgh 1777, pp350, 351. On the contrary, lowness of wages produces in its turn, dearness of labour. 'Labour being dearer in Ireland than it is in England ... because the wages are so much lower', N. 2074 in 'Royal Commission on Railways, Minutes,' 1867.

3. A Ure, *The Philosophy of Manufacturers*, London 1835, p314.

4. H. Carey, 'Essay on the Rate of Wages: with an Examination of the Causes of the Differences in the Condition of the Labouring Population throughout the world', Philadelphia 1835.

18

FORMATION OF SUPPLY IN GENERAL

During its existence as commodity capital or its stay in the market, in other words, during the interval between the process of production, from which it emerges, and the process of consumption, into which it enters, the product constitutes a commodity supply. As a commodity in the market, and therefore in the shape of a supply, commodity capital figures in a dual capacity in each circuit: one time as the commodity product of that capital in process whose circuit is being examined; the other time however as the commodity product of another capital, which must be available in the market to be bought and converted into productive capital. It is, indeed, possible that this last-named commodity capital is not produced until ordered. In that event an interruption occurs until it has been produced. But the flow of the process of production and reproduction requires that a certain mass of commodities (means of production) should always be in the market, should therefore form a supply. Productive capital likewise comprises the purchase of labour power, and the money form is here only the value form of the means of subsistence, the greater part of which the labourer must find at hand in the market. We shall discuss this more in detail further on in this paragraph. But at this point the following is already clear. As far as concerns capital value in process which has been transformed into a commodity and must now be sold or reconverted into money, which therefore functions for the moment as commodity capital in the market, the condition in which it constitutes a supply is to be described as an inexpedient, involuntary stay there. The quicker the sale is effected the more smoothly runs the process of reproduction. Delay in the form conversion of C′ – M′ impedes the real exchange of matter which must take place in the circuit of capital, as well as its further functioning as productive capital. On the other hand, so far as M – C is concerned, the constant presence of commodities in the market, commodity supply, appears as a condition of the flow of the process of reproduction and of the investment of new or additional capital.

The abidance of the commodity capital as a commodity supply in the market requires buildings, stores, storage places, warehouses, in other words, an expenditure of constant capital; furthermore the payment of labour power for placing the commodities in storage. Besides, commodities spoil and are exposed to the injurious influences of the elements. Additional capital must be invested, partly in instruments of labour, in an objectified form, and partly in labour power to protect the commodities against the above.[1]

Thus the existence of capital in its form of commodity capital and hence of commodity supply gives rise to costs which must be classed as costs of circulation, since they do not come within the sphere of production. These costs of circulation differ from those mentioned under I[2] by the fact that they enter to a certain extent into the value of the commodities, i.e., they increase the prices of commodities. At all events the capital and labour power which serve the need of preserving and storing the commodity supply are withdrawn from the direct process of production. On the other hand the capitals thus employed, including labour power as a constituent of capital, must be replaced out of the social product. Their expenditure has therefore the effect of diminishing the productive power of labour, so that a greater amount of capital and labour is required to obtain a particular useful effect. They are *unproductive costs*.

As the costs of circulation necessitated by the formation of a commodity supply are due merely to the time required for the conversion of existing values from the commodity form into the money form, hence merely to the particular social form of the production process (i.e., are due only to the fact that the product is brought forth as a commodity and must therefore undergo the transformation into money), these costs completely share the character of the circulation costs enumerated under I.[3] On the other hand the value of the commodities is here preserved or increased only because the use value, the product itself, is placed in definite objective conditions which cost capital outlay, and is subjected to operations which bring additional labour to bear on the use values. However the computation of the values of commodities, the bookkeeping incidental to this process, the transactions of purchase and sale, do not affect the use value in which the commodity value exists. They have to do only with the form of the commodity value. Although in the case submitted here[4] the costs of forming a supply (which is here done involuntarily) arise only from a delay in the change of form and from its necessity, [...] their purpose is not a change in the form of the value, but the preservation of the value existing in the commodity as a product, a utility, and which cannot be preserved in any other way than by preserving the product, the use value, itself. The use value is neither raised nor increased here; on the contrary, it diminishes. But its diminution is restricted and it is preserved. Neither is the advanced value contained in the commodity increased here; but new labour, objectified and living, is added.

We have now to investigate furthermore to what extent these costs arise from the peculiar nature of commodity production in general and from commodity production in its general, absolute form, i.e., capitalist commodity production; and to what extent on the other hand they are common to all social production and merely assume a special shape, a special form of appearance, in capitalist production.

Adam Smith entertained the splendid notion that the formation of a supply was a phenomenon peculiar to capitalist production.[5] More recent economists, for instance Lalor, insist on the contrary that it declines with the development of capitalist production. Sismondi even regards it as one of the drawbacks of the latter.

As a matter of fact, supplies exist in three forms: in the form of productive capital, in the form of a fund for individual consumption, and in the form of a commodity supply or commodity capital. The supply in one form decreases relatively when it increases in another, although its quantity may increase absolutely in all three forms simultaneously.

It is plain from the outset that wherever production is carried on for the direct satisfaction of the needs of the producer and only to a minor extent for exchange or sale, hence where the social product does not assume the form of commodities at all or only to a rather small degree, the supply in the form of commodities, or commodity supply, forms only a small and insignificant part of wealth. But here the consumption fund is relatively large, especially that of the means of subsistence proper. One need but take a look at old-fashioned peasant economy. Here the overwhelming part of the product is transformed directly into supplies of means of production or means of subsistence, without becoming supplies of commodities, for the very reason that it remains in the hands of its owner. It does not assume the form of a commodity supply and for this reason Adam Smith declares that there is no supply in societies based on this mode of production. He confuses the form of the supply with the supply itself and believes that society hitherto lived from hand to mouth or trusted to the hap of the morrow.[6] This is a naïve misunderstanding.

A supply in the form of productive capital exists in the shape of means of production, which are already in the process of production or at least in the hands of the producer, hence latently already in the process of production. It was seen previously that with the development of the productivity of labour and therefore also with the development of the capitalist mode of production – which develops the social productive power of labour more than all previous modes of production – there is a steady increase in the mass of means of production (buildings, machinery, etc.) which are incorporated once and for all in the process in the form of instruments of labour, and perform with steady repetition their function in it for a longer or shorter time. It was also observed that this increase is at the same time the premise and consequence of the development of the social productive power of labour. The growth, not only absolute but also relative, of wealth in this form is characteristic above all of the capitalist mode of production.[7] The material forms of existence of constant capital, the means of production, do not however consist only of such instruments of labour but also of materials of labour in various stages of processing, and of auxiliary materials. With the enlargement of the scale of production and the increase in the productive power of labour through co-operation, division of labour, machinery, etc., grows the quantity of raw materials, auxiliary materials, etc., entering into the daily process of reproduction.

These elements must be ready at hand at the place of production. The volume of this supply existing in the form of productive capital increases therefore absolutely. In order that the process may keep going – apart from the fact whether this supply can be renewed daily or only at fixed intervals – there must always be a greater accumulation of ready raw material, etc., at the place of production than is used up, say, daily or weekly. The continuity of the process requires that the presence of its conditions should not be jeopardised by possible interruptions when making purchases daily, nor depend on whether the product is sold daily or weekly, and hence is reconvertible into its elements of production only irregularly. But it is evident that productive capital may be latent or form a supply in quite different proportions. There is for instance a great difference whether a spinning-mill owner must have on hand a supply of cotton or coal for three months or for one. Patently this supply, while increasing absolutely, may decrease relatively.

This depends on various conditions, all of which practically amount to a demand for greater rapidity, regularity, and reliability in furnishing the necessary amount of raw material, so that no interruption will ever occur. The less these conditions are complied with, hence the less rapid, regular, and reliable the supplies, the greater must be the latent part of the productive capital, that is to say, the supply of raw material, etc., in the hands of the producer, waiting to be worked up. These conditions are inversely proportional to the degree of development of capitalist production, and hence of the productive power of social labour. The same applies therefore to the supply in this form.

However that which appears here as a decrease of the supply (for instance, in labour) is in part merely a decrease of the supply in the form of commodity capital, or of the commodity supply proper; it is consequently only a change of form of the same supply. If for instance a great quantity of coal is produced every day in a certain country, and therefore the scale and the energy of operation of the coal industry are great, the spinner does not need a large store of coal in order to ensure the continuity of his production. The steady and certain renewal of the coal supply makes this unnecessary. In the second place the rapidity with which the product of one process may be transferred as means of production to another process depends on the development of the transport and communication facilities. The cheapness of transportation is of great importance in this question. The continually renewed transport of coal from the mine to the spinning-mill for instance would be more expensive than the storing up of a larger supply of coal for a longer time when the price of transportation is relatively cheaper. These two circumstances examined so far arise from the process of production itself. In the third place the development of the credit system also exerts an influence. The less the spinner is dependent on the direct sale of his yarn for the renewal of his supply of cotton, coal, etc. – and this direct dependence will be the smaller, the more developed the credit system is – the smaller relatively these supplies can be and yet ensure a continuous production of yarn on a given scale, a production independent of the hazards of the sale of yarn. In the fourth place, however, many raw materials, semi-finished goods, etc., require rather long periods of time for their production. This applies especially to all raw materials furnished by agriculture. If no interruption of the process of production is to take place, a certain amount of raw materials must be on hand for the entire period in which no new products can take the place of the old. If this supply decreases in the hands of the industrial capitalist, it proves merely that it increases in the hands of the merchant in the form of commodity supply. The development of transportation for instance makes it possible rapidly to ship the cotton lying, say, in Liverpool's import warehouses to Manchester, so that the manufacturer can renew his supply in comparatively small portions, as and when needed. But in that case the cotton remains in so much larger quantities as commodity supply in the hands of the Liverpool merchants. It is therefore merely a change in the form of the supply, and this Lalor and others overlooked. And if you consider the social capital, the same quantity of products exists in either case in the form of supply. The quantity required for a single country during the period of, say, one year decreases as transportation improves. If a large number of sailing vessels and steamers ply between America and England, England's opportunities to renew its cotton supply are increased while the average quantity to be held in storage in England decreases. The same effect is produced by the development of the world market and the consequent multiplication of the sources of supply of the same merchandise. The article is supplied piecemeal from various countries and at various intervals.

NOTES

1. Corbet calculates, in 1841, that the cost of storing wheat for a season of nine months amounts to a loss of ½ per cent for delivery, together 7 per cent, or 3s. 6d. on a price of 50s. per quarter, Th. Corbet, *An Inquiry into the Causes and Modes of the Wealth of Individuals, etc.*, London 1841, [p140]22. According to the testimony of Liverpool merchants before the Railway Commission, the (net) costs of grain storage in 1865 amounted to about 2d. per quarter per month, or 9d. or 10d. a ton, *Royal Commission on Railways*, 1867. Evidence, p19, No. 331.
2. See 'The Costs of Circulation: I. Genuine Costs of Circulation', *MECW* vol. 36, pp133-140, Lawrence and Wishart, London 1997. [Ed.]
3. See note 2.
4. i.e., Corbet's calculations given in Footnote 1.
5. Book II, Introduction, A. Smith, *An Inquiry into the Nature and Causes of the Wealth of Nations*.
6. Instead of a supply arising only upon and from the conversion of the product into a commodity, and of the consumption supply into a commodity supply, as Adam Smith wrongly imagines, this change of form, on the contrary, causes most violent crises in the economy of the producers during the transition from production for one's own needs to commodity production. In India, for instance, 'the disposition to hoard largely the grain for which little could be got in years of abundance' was observed until very recent times, *Return. Bengal and Orissa Famine, H of C, 1867*, I, pp230-231, No. 74. The sudden increase in the demand for cotton, jute, etc., due to the American Civil War, led in many parts of India to a severe restriction of rice culture, a rise in the price of rice, and a sale of the producers' old rice supplies. To this must be added the unexampled export of rice to Australia, Madagascar, etc., in 1864-66. This accounts for the acute character of the famine of 1866, which cost the lives of a million people in the district of Orissa alone.
7. See *MECW* vol. 35, Lawrence and Wishart, London 1996. [*Ed.*]

Section 8: Capital, finance and profit

19. Karl Marx, 'Money Capital and Real Capital', from *Capital 3* (1894), *Marx and Engels Collected Works*, vol. 37, pp475-484

20. Karl Marx, 'Decline in the Rate of Profit', from *Economic Manuscripts* (1861-3), *Marx and Engels Collected Works*, vol. 33, pp148-151

Many people who believe that globalisation is under way argue that capitalism is changing, and that different sectors of the world economy are becoming more significant than others. The financial capital which can be tracked through currency deals and on the trading floors, is already mobile, indeed 'global' in its reach. Yet for all the recent trends towards outsourcing, industrial capital requires individual units of production. It is still impossible to move machines at the speed with which shares are traded. So globalisation theory must suggest that financial capital is becoming increasingly important, while industrial capital declines. Whether this is true today or not, Marx was extremely sceptical of the equivalent theories, when they were expressed over a hundred years ago. The first passage in this section is taken from *Capital, Volume 3*, in which Marx argues that under conditions of advanced capitalism, finance is generally subordinate to industry. Where was his evidence? – in the timing of business slumps, which followed the highs and lows of the industrial cycle. Industry dominated trade, and not the other way around.

The second extract in this section summarises Marx's belief that there was a general tendency for the rate of profit to fall. *Capital 3* elaborates this claim, although the passage here is actually taken from the draft notes which were used to construct the longer book. The notion of a declining rate of profit follows on from Karl Marx's opinion that the only source of value was human labour. If one company was to steal a march on its rivals, then one obvious way to do this would be to ask 'their' workforce to work harder. But in a competitive market, everyone else would do this as well. So the most common way to achieve relative success was by introducing new machinery. If ten workers could complete a task where previously fifty were required, then that company would profit in relation to its rivals. The social weight of labour would increase, and more value would be introduced. The problem would come when every single company was constantly investing in new technology – as they do. Then Marx argued, the general trend would be for a much greater increase in investment on machinery, with relatively-less investment in labour. The general rate of profit would fall. The model of capitalism which follows from this passage is of a system which ages and goes into decline.

19

MONEY CAPITAL AND REAL CAPITAL

The only difficult questions, which we are now approaching in connection with the credit system, are the following:

First: The accumulation of the actual money capital. To what extent is it, and to what extent is it not, an indication of an actual accumulation of capital, i.e., of reproduction on an extended scale? Is the so-called PLETHORA of capital – an expression used only with reference to the interest-bearing capital, i.e., money capital – only a special way of expressing industrial overproduction, or does it constitute a separate phenomenon alongside of it? Does this PLETHORA, or excessive supply of money capital, coincide with the existence of stagnating masses of money (bullion, gold coin and banknotes), so that this super-abundance of actual money is the expression and external form of that PLETHORA of loan capital?

Secondly: To what extent does a scarcity of money, i.e., a shortage of loan capital, express a shortage of real capital (commodity capital and productive capital)? To what extent does it coincide, on the other hand, with a shortage of money as such, a shortage of the medium of circulation?

In so far as we have hitherto considered the peculiar form of accumulation of money capital and of money wealth in general, it has resolved itself into an accumulation of claims of ownership upon labour. The accumulation of the capital of the national debt has been revealed to mean merely an increase in a class of state creditors, who have the privilege of a firm claim upon a certain portion of the tax revenue.[1] By means of these facts, whereby even an accumulation of debts may appear as an accumulation of capital, the height of distortion taking place in the credit system becomes apparent. These promissory notes, which are issued for the originally loaned capital long since spent, these paper duplicates of consumed capital, serve for their owners as capital to the extent that they are saleable commodities and may, therefore, be reconverted into capital.

Titles of ownership to public works, railways, mines, etc., are indeed, as we have also seen, titles to real capital. But they do not place this capital at one's disposal. It is not subject to withdrawal. They merely convey legal claims to a portion of the surplus value to be obtained by it. But these titles likewise become paper duplicates of the real capital; it is as though a bill of lading were to acquire a value separate from the cargo, both concomitantly and simultaneously with it. They come to nominally represent non-existent capital. For the real capital exists side by side with them and does not change hands as a result of the transfer of these duplicates from one person to another. They assume the form of interest-bearing capital, not only because they guarantee a certain income, but also because, through their sale, their repayment as capital values can be obtained. To the extent that the accumulation of this paper expresses the accumulation of railways, mines, steamships, etc., to that extent does it express the extension of the actual reproduction process – just as the extension of, for example, a tax list on movable property indicates the expansion of this property. But as duplicates which are themselves objects of transactions as commodities, and thus able to circulate as capital values, they are illusory, and their value may fall or rise quite independently of the movement of value of the real capital for which they are titles. Their value, that is, their quotation on the Stock Exchange, necessarily has a tendency to rise with a fall in the rate of interest – in so far as this fall, independent of the characteristic movements of money capital, is due merely to the tendency for the rate of profit to fall; therefore, this imaginary wealth expands, if for this reason alone, in the course of capitalist production in accordance with the expressed value for each of its aliquot parts of specific original nominal value.[2]

Gain and loss through fluctuations in the price of these titles of ownership, and their centralisation in the hands of railway kings, etc., become, by their very nature, more and more a matter of gamble, which appears to take the place of labour as the original method of acquiring capital wealth and also replaces naked force. This type of imaginary money wealth not only constitutes a very considerable part of the money wealth of private people, but also of banker's capital, as we have already indicated.

In order to quickly settle this question, let us point out that one could also mean by the accumulation of money capital the accumulation of wealth in the hands of bankers (money lenders by profession), acting as middlemen between private money capitalists on the one hand, and the state, communities, and reproducing borrowers on the other. For the entire vast extension of the credit system, and all credit in general, is exploited by them as their private capital. These fellows always possess capital and incomes in money form or in direct claims on money. The accumulation of the wealth of this class may take place completely differently than actual accumulation, but it proves at any rate that this class pockets a good deal of the real accumulation.

Let us reduce the scope of the problem before us. Government securities, like stocks and other securities of all kinds, are spheres of investment for loanable capital – capital intended for bearing interest. They are forms of loaning such capital. But they themselves are not the loan capital, which is invested in them. On the other hand, in so far as credit plays a direct role in the reproduction process, what the industrialist or merchant needs when he wishes to have a bill discounted or a loan granted is neither stocks nor government securities. What he needs is money. He, therefore, pledges or sells those securities if he cannot secure money in any other way. It is the accumulation of *this* loan capital with which we have to deal here, and more particularly accumulation of loanable money capital. We are not concerned here with loans of houses, machines, or other fixed capital. Nor are we concerned with the advances industrialists and merchants make to one another in commodities and within the compass of the reproduction process; although we must also investigate this point beforehand in more detail. We are concerned exclusively with money loans, which are made by bankers, as middlemen, to industrialists and merchants.

Let us then, to begin with, analyse commercial credit, that is, the credit which the capitalists engaged in reproduction give to one another. It forms the basis of the credit system. It is represented by the bill of exchange, a promissory note with a definite term of payment, i.e., a DOCUMENT OF DEFERRED PAYMENT. Let us completely disregard, for the present, banker's credit, which constitutes an entirely different sphere. To the extent that these bills of exchange circulate among the merchants themselves as means of payment again, by endorsement from one to another – without, however, the mediation of discounting – it is merely a transfer of the claim from A to B and does not change the picture in the least. It merely replaces one person by another. And even in this case, the liquidation can take place without the intervention of money. Spinner A, for example, has to pay a bill to cotton broker B, and the latter to importer C. Now, if C also exports yarn, which happens often enough, he may buy yarn from A on a bill of exchange and the spinner A may pay the broker B with the broker's own bill which was received in payment from C. At most, a balance will have to be paid in money. The entire transaction then consists merely in the exchange of cotton and yarn. The exporter represents only the spinner, and the cotton broker, the cotton planter.

Two things are now to be noted in the circuit of this purely commercial credit.

First: The settlement of these mutual claims depends upon the return flow of capital, that is, on C – M, which is merely deferred. If the spinner has received a bill of exchange from a cotton goods manufacturer, the manufacturer can pay if the cotton goods which he has on the market have been sold in the interim. If the corn speculator has a bill of exchange drawn upon his agent, the agent can pay the money if the corn has been sold in the interim at the expected price. These payments, therefore, depend on the fluidity of reproduction, that is, the production and consumption processes. But since the credits are mutual, the solvency of one depends upon the solvency of another; for in drawing his bill of exchange, one may have counted either on the return flow of the capital in his own business or on the return flow of the capital in a third party's business whose bill of exchange is due in the meantime.

Aside from the prospect of the return flow of capital, payment can only be possible by means of reserve capital at the disposal of the person drawing the bill of exchange, in order to meet his obligations in case the return flow of capital should be delayed.

Secondly: This credit system does not do away with the necessity for cash payments. For one thing, a large portion of expenses must always be paid in cash, e.g., wages, taxes, etc. Furthermore, capitalist B, who has received from C a bill of exchange in place of cash payment, may have to pay a bill of his own which has fallen due to D before C's bill becomes due, and so he must have ready cash. A complete circuit of reproduction as that assumed above, i.e., from cotton planter to cotton spinner and back again, can only constitute an exception; it will be constantly interrupted at many points. We have seen in the discussion of the reproduction process that the producers of constant capital exchange, in part, constant capital among themselves.[3] As a result, the bills of exchange can, more or less, balance each other out. Similarly, in the ascending line of production, where the cotton broker draws on the cotton spinner, the spinner on the manufacturer of cotton goods, the manufacturer on the exporter, the exporter on the importer (perhaps of cotton again). But the circuit of transactions, and, therefore, the turn about of the series of claims, does not take place at the same time. For example, the claim of the spinner on the weaver is not settled by the claim on the coal-dealer on the machine-builder. The spinner never has any counter-claims on the machine-builder, in his business, because his product, yarn, never enters as an element in the machine-builder's reproduction process. Such claims must, therefore, be settled by money.

The limits of this commercial credit, considered by themselves, are 1) the wealth of the industrialists and merchants, that is, their command of reserve capital in case of delayed returns; 2) these returns themselves. These returns may be delayed, or the price of commodities may fall in the meantime of the commodities may become momentarily unsaleable due to a stagnant market. The longer the bills of exchange run, the larger must be the reserve capital, and the greater the possibility of a diminution or delay of the returns through a fall in prices or a glut on the market. And, furthermore, the returns are so much less secure, the more the original transaction was conditioned upon speculation on the rise or fall of commodity prices. But it is evident that with the development of the productive power of labour, and thus of production on a large scale: 1) the markets expand and become more distant from the place of production; 2) credits must, therefore, be prolonged; 3) the speculative element must thus more and more dominate the transactions. Production on a large scale and for distant markets throws the total product into the hands of commerce; but it is impossible that the capital of a nation should double itself in such a manner that commerce should itself be able to buy up the entire national product with its own capital and to sell it again. Credit is, therefore, indispensable here; credit, whose volume grows with the growing volume of value of production and whose time duration grows with the increasing distance of the markets. A mutual interaction takes place here. The development of the production process extends the credit, and credit leads to an extension of industrial and commercial operations.

When we examine this credit detached from banker's credit, it is evident that it grows with an increasing volume of industrial capital itself. Loan capital and industrial capital are identical here. The loaned capital is commodity capital which is intended either for ultimate individual consumption or for the replacement of the constant elements of productive capital. What appears here as loan capital is always capital existing in some definite phase of the reproduction process, but which by means of purchase and sale passes from one person to another, while its equivalent is not paid by the buyer until some later stipulated time. For example, cotton is transferred to the spinner for a bill of exchange, yarn to the manufacturer of cotton goods for a bill of exchange, cotton goods to the merchant for a bill, from whose hands they go to the exporter for a bill, and then, for a bill to some merchant in India, who sells the goods and buys indigo instead, etc. During this transfer from hand to hand the transformation of cotton into cotton goods is effected, and the cotton goods are finally transported to India and exchanged for indigo, which is shipped to Europe and there enters into the reproduction process again. The various phases of the reproduction process are promoted here by credit, without any payment on the part of the spinner for the cotton, the manufacturer of cotton goods for the yarn, the merchant for the cotton goods, etc. In the first stages of the process, the commodity, cotton, goes through its various production phases, and this transition is promoted by credit. But as soon as the cotton has received in production its ultimate form as a commodity, the same commodity capital passes only through the hands of various merchants who promote its transportation to distant markets, and the last of whom finally sells these commodities to the consumer and buys other commodities in their stead, which either become consumed or go into the reproduction process. It is necessary, then, to differentiate between two stages here: in the first stage, credit promotes the actual successive phases in the production of the same article; in the second, credit merely promotes the transfer of the article, including its transportation, from one merchant to another, in other words, the process C – M. But here also the commodity is at least in the act of circulation, that is, in a phase of the reproduction process.

It follows, then, that it is never idle capital which is loaned here, but capital which must change its form in the hands of its owner; it exists in a form that for him is merely commodity capital, i.e., capital which must be retransformed, and, to begin with, at least converted into money. It is, therefore, the metamorphosis of commodities that is here promoted by credit; not merely C – M, but also M – C and the actual production process. A large quantity of credit within the reproductive circuit (banker's credit excepted) does not signify a large quantity of idle capital, which is being offered for loan and is seeking profitable investment. It means rather a large employment of capital in the reproduction process. Credit, then, promotes here 1) as far as the industrial capitalists are concerned, the transition of industrial capital from one phase into another, the connection of related and dovetailing spheres of production; 2) as far as the merchants are concerned, the transportation and transition of commodities from one person to another until their definite sale for money or their exchange for other commodities.

The maximum of credit is here identical with the fullest employment of industrial capital, that is, the utmost exertion of its reproductive power without regard to the limits of consumption. These limits of consumption are extended by the exertions of the reproduction process itself. On the one hand, this increases the consumption of revenue on the part of labourers and capitalists, on the other hand, it is identical with an exertion of productive consumption.

As long as the reproduction process is continuous and, therefore, the return flow assured, this credit exists and expands, and its expansion is based upon the expansion of the reproduction process itself. As soon as a stoppage takes place, as a result of delayed returns, glutted markets, or fallen prices, a superabundance of industrial capital becomes available, but in a form in which it cannot perform its functions. Huge quantities of commodity capital, but unsaleable. Huge quantities of fixed capital, but largely idle due to stagnant reproduction. Credit is contracted 1) because this capital is idle, i.e., blocked in one of its phases of reproduction because it cannot complete its metamorphosis; 2) because confidence in the continuity of the reproduction process has been shaken; 3) because the demand for this commercial credit diminishes. The spinner, who curtails his production and has a large quantity of unsold yarn in stock, does not need to buy any cotton on credit; the merchant does not need to buy any commodities on credit because he has more than enough of them.

Hence, if there is a disturbance in this expansion or even in the normal flow of the reproduction process, credit also becomes scarce; it is more difficult to obtain commodities on credit. However, the demand for cash payment and the caution observed toward sales on credit are particularly characteristic of the phase of the industrial cycle following a crash. During the crisis itself, since everyone has products to sell, cannot sell them, and yet must sell them in order to meet payments, it is not the mass of idle and investment-seeking capital, but rather the mass of capital impeded in its reproduction process, that is greatest just when the shortage of credit is most acute (and therefore the rate of discount highest for banker's credit). The capital already invested is then, indeed, idle in large quantities because the reproduction process is stagnant. Factories are closed, raw materials accumulate, finished products flood the market as commodities. Nothing is more erroneous, therefore, than to blame a scarcity of productive capital for such a condition. It is precisely at such times that there is a superabundance of productive capital, partly in relation to the normal, but temporarily reduced scale of reproduction, and partly in relation to the paralysed consumption.

Let us suppose that the whole of society is composed only of industrial capitalists and wage workers. Let us furthermore disregard price fluctuations, which prevent large portions of the total capital from replacing themselves in their average proportions and which, owing to the general interrelations of the entire reproduction process as developed in particular by credit, must always call forth general stoppages of a transient nature. Let us also disregard the sham transactions and speculations, which the credit system favours. Then, a crisis could only be explained as the result of a disproportion of production in various branches of the economy, and as a result of a disproportion between the consumption of the capitalists and their accumulation. But as matters stand, the replacement of the capital invested in production depends largely upon the consuming power of the non-producing classes; while the consuming power of the workers is limited partly by the laws of wages, partly by the fact that they are used only as long as they can be profitably employed by the capitalist class. The ultimate reason for all real crises always remains the poverty and restricted consumption of the masses as opposed to the drive of capitalist production to develop the productive forces as though only the absolute consuming power of society constituted their limit.

A real lack of productive capital, at least among capitalistically developed nations, can be said to exist only in times of general crop failures, either in the principal foodstuffs or in the principal industrial raw materials.

However, in addition to this commercial credit we have actual money credit. The advances of the industrialists and merchants among one another are amalgamated with the money advances made to them by the bankers and money lenders. In discounting bills of exchange the advance is only nominal. A manufacturer sells his product for a bill of exchange and gets this bill discounted by some BILL-BROKER. In reality, the latter advances only the credit of his banker, who in turn advances to the broker the money capital of his depositors. The depositors consist of the industrialists and merchants themselves and also of workers (through savings banks) – as well as ground rent recipients and other unproductive classes. In this way every individual industrial manufacturer and merchant gets around the necessity of keeping a large reserve capital and being dependent upon his actual returns. On the other hand, the whole process becomes so complicated, partly by simply manipulating bills of exchange, partly by commodity transactions for the sole purpose of manufacturing bills of exchange, that the semblance of a very solvent business with a smooth flow of returns can easily persist even long after returns actually come in only at the expense partly of swindled money lenders and partly of swindled producers. Thus business always appears almost excessively sound right on the eve of a crash. The best proof of this is furnished, for instance, by the Reports on Bank Acts of 1857 and 1858, in which all bank directors, merchants, in short all the invited experts with Lord Overstone at their head, congratulated one another on the prosperity and soundness of business – just one month before the outbreak of the crisis in August 1857.[4] And, strangely enough, Tooke in his *History of Prices* succumbs to this illusion once again as historian for each crisis.[5] Business is always thoroughly sound and the campaign in full swing, until suddenly the debacle takes place.

NOTES

1. 'The public fund is nothing but imaginary capital, which represents that portion of the annual revenue, which is set aside to pay the debt. An equivalent amount of capital has been spent; it is this which serves as a denominator for the loan, but it is not this which is represented by the public fund; for the capital no longer exists. New wealth must be created by the work of industry; a portion of this wealth is annually set aside in advance for those who have loaned that wealth which has been spent; this portion is taken by means of taxes from those who produce it, and is given to the creditors of the state, and, according to the customary proportion between capital and interest in the country, an imaginary capital is assumed equivalent to that which could give rise to the annual income which these

creditors are to receive', Sismondi, *Nouveaux principes*, second edition, Paris 1827, p230.

2.   A portion of the accumulated loanable money capital is indeed merely an expression of industrial capital. For instance, when England, in 1857, had invested £80 million in American railways and other enterprises, this investment was transacted almost completely by the export of English commodities for which the Americans did not have to make payment in return. The English exporter drew bills of exchange for these commodities on America, which the English stock subscribers bought up and which were sent to America for purchasing the stock subscriptions.

3.   See *MECW* vol. 36, Lawrence and Wishart, London 1997. [*Ed.*]

4.   See Report from the Select Committee on Bank Acts, Part I, 1857, pp327-419.

5.   Th. Tooke, *A History of Prices, and of the State of the Circulation, from 1839 to 1847 Inclusive*, pp329-348 and *A History of Prices, and of the State of the Circulation, During the Nine Years 1848-1856*, Vol. VI, pp218-229.

20

DECLINE IN THE RATE OF PROFIT

The result of the investigation is this: Firstly, the rate of surplus value does not rise in proportion to the growth in productive power or the decline in the (relative) number of workers employed. The capital does not grow in the same proportion as the productive power. Or, the rate of surplus value does not rise in the same proportion as the variable capital falls in comparison with the total amount of capital. Hence, a diminution in the relative magnitude of the surplus value. Hence *a decline in the rate of profit. A constant tendency towards a decline in the same.*

It should be remarked further on this point that the law whereby the value of the commodities is determined by the labour time socially necessary for their production drive the individual capitalist, so that he can sell his commodity *above* its social value, to curtail the labour time necessary for him exceptionally by introducing the division of labour, by employing machinery, etc – also in spheres of production whose products enter neither directly nor indirectly into the worker's consumption or into the conditions of production of his articles of consumption – therefore also in branches of production where no development of productive power can cheapen the reproduction of labour capacity, i.e. shorten the necessary labour time and lengthen the surplus labour time. Once proof has actually been provided that these commodities can be produced more cheaply, the capitalists who work under the old conditions of production must sell them *below* the value, since the labour time they need for the production of those commodities now stands *above* the labour time socially *necessary* for their production. In a word – and this appears as an effect of competition – they too must adopt the new mode of production, in which the ratio of the variable capital to the total amount of capital advanced has fallen. Here, therefore, there takes place a reduction in the value of the commodities, and a reduction in the number of workers exploited, without an increase of any kind in relative surplus value. This situation in the unproductive spheres of production – those not producing relative surplus value – is of substantial influence, if one considers the capital of the whole society, i.e., of the capitalist class, from the angle that the total amount of surplus value falls in proportion to the capital advanced – hence that the *rate of profit* falls.

It is possible that such commodities may by growing cheaper become accessible to the workers' consumption, may indeed become necessary elements in this. Their effect is never direct, and is never more than partial. They DIVERSIFY its magnitude without raising its value. Above all, they DIVERSIFY the magnitude of the capitalists' [consumption], a point which can be made for any development in productivity, but which is irrelevant in our context. They even exert an economic influence, in so far as every expansion of the sphere of exchange, every magnification of the number of stages in which the exchange value of a commodity unfolds promotes at the same time its character as commodity, hence also promotes the mode of production directed exclusively at the production of *commodities*, not of use values as such.

On the other hand, the fall in variable capital in comparison with total capital – and this fall accompanies every development of productive power – does not occur to the same degree as productive power develops, because an ever more considerable portion of the capital enters into the value of the commodities, into the valorisation process, only in the form of annuities, and because during certain periods a constant increase takes place in the size of the capital in the production of a particular commodity without accompanying changes in the ratio of the organic components, i.e., it remains on the basis of the old mode of production. The rate of profit therefore does not diminish in the same proportion as capital grows (still less in a greater proportion), although the growth of capital – to the extent that it depends on the development of the productive forces – is continuously accompanied by a tendential fall in the rate of profit.

We therefore say, on the one hand: capital does not grow as quickly as productive power. We say, on the other hand: the rate of profit does not fall as quickly as capital grows. We say, on the one hand: variable capital does not decline as quickly in proportion to total capital, or total capital does not grow as quickly in proportion to variable capital, as productivity grows. We say, on the other hand: the surplus value created by variable capital does not grow as quickly as the variable capital falls, and does not fall as quickly as the constant capital rises. (Of the total capital).

The absolute magnitude of surplus value declines, in comparison with the capital advanced, although the rate of surplus value rises, with the fall in variable capital, or in the relative portion of the total capital which is laid out in wages. But it declines more slowly than variable capital falls. The rate of profit therefore does not fall as quickly as the total capital grows. On the other hand, the total capital does not grow as quickly as productive power and the replacement of variable capital by constant capital which accompanies this. This would therefore imply that variable capital falls more quickly than the total capital grows. But this is incorrect, in so far as the total capital enters into the valorisation process. However, the more rapid growth in the productive power of capital means only that the growth in the rate of surplus value does not correspond to the growth in productive power.

In so far as the employment of a greater amount of constant capital really creates [greater] surplus value, the aliquot part of the total amount of capital which corresponds to a single worker must be smaller than the total amount of capital which corresponded to the number of workers he replaces. But this comparative reduction in the aliquot parts of the capital relative to the individual workers employed by it (absolutely greater in relation to this individual, smaller in relation to the number he replaces) generally occurs – and in the further course of development always occurs – with a simultaneous increase in the absolute size of the capital, hence of the sum total of these aliquot parts. If, e.g., a capital of 400 was used for one instead of 500 for 20, these 400 could perhaps only be employed in this manner if 10,000x400 were employed. Therefore, although the conditions of labour would be cheaper for the individual worker – not compared with the previous individual worker, but with the previous 20 workers – there is a rise in the total value of the conditions of labour which must be possessed by the individual so as to carry on the productive labour process under these new conditions. I.e., the power of capital vis-à-vis labour grows, or, and this is the same thing, the worker's chance of appropriating the conditions of labour for himself is lessened. The independent position of past labour as an alien power over living labour achieves a tremendous extension of its dimensions. The good Carey overlooked this. The single spindle is cheaper, but the workshop needed to employ mechanical spindles of this kind requires a capital extraordinarily increased in size, compared with that required previously by the hand spinner.

At the start of developments in many spheres of production where the tool is transformed into a machine of labour – but has not yet developed into a system of machinery – there may indeed be a fall in the amount of capital required, if e.g., 1 worker replaces 10, the raw material remains the same, and the cost of the machine-like tool is in contrast less than the wages of the 10 workers over one year. Mr Carey TAKES HOLD OF such phenomena of the transition from manual to machine labour TO MAKE A FOOL OF HIMSELF. But these small machines are then seized upon by capital, which applies to them the principles of co-operation and the division of labour, and the principle of the proportional reduction of production costs, and finally subjects the whole workshop to a motivating machine or a natural force.

Section 9: Labour

21. Karl Marx, 'Contradictions of Big Industry: Revolution', based on *The German Ideology* (1845), *Marx and Engels Collected Works*, vol. 5, pp85-89; the translation here is taken from Karl Marx, *The German Ideology: Student edition*, C.J. Arthur (ed), Lawrence and Wishart, London 1974, pp91-5.

Faced with the reality of a world dominated by international capital, Marx and Engels refused to champion national capital instead. As far as they were concerned, the problem with capitalist internationalisation was not that it was international – but that it was capitalist. Their alternative was the international of labour, a society organised by and for workers, which could only be built on the basis of international solidarity in struggle. Elsewhere, this notion was expressed in the famous concluding sentences of *The Communist Manifesto*, 'Workers of the world, unite'.

The German Ideology was written in 1845-6, but not published in Marx's lifetime. It was the first systematic statement of the materialist conception of history. Written in rejection of the crude materialism of Feuerbach – hence the title – Marx argued that the 'real basis of ideology' could be found in the historic experience of the eighteenth and nineteenth centuries, the rise of capitalist trade and industry. This extract follows a discussion (in the original) of the rise of big industry, and the role of conquest in history. Marx argued that the growth of capital created unexpected consequences. Labour was concentrated in cities, becoming the majority of the population. But workers were unreliable, they lacked the property that would determine their loyalty to the system. Capitalism required labour, without workers the machines would run idle. But workers did not require employers to produce. All in all, big business was creating the conditions for its own destruction.

21

CONTRADICTIONS OF BIG INDUSTRY: REVOLUTION

Our investigation hitherto started from the instruments of production, and it has already shown that private property was a necessity for certain industrial stages. In *industrie extractive* private property still coincides with labour; in small industry and all agriculture up till now property is the necessary consequence of the existing instruments of production; in big industry the contradiction between the instrument of production and private property appears from the first time and is the product of big industry; moreover, big industry must be highly developed to produce this contradiction. And thus only with big industry does the abolition of private property become possible.

In big industry and competition the whole mass of conditions of existence, limitations, biases of individuals, are fused together into the two simplest forms: private property and labour. With money every form of intercourse, and intercourse itself, is considered fortuitous for the individuals. Thus money implies that all previous intercourse was only intercourse of individuals under particular conditions, not of individuals as individuals. These conditions are reduced to two: accumulated labour or private property, and actual labour. If both or one of these ceases, then intercourse comes to a standstill. The modern economists themselves, e.g. Sismondi, Cherbuliez, etc., oppose 'association of individuals' to 'association of capital'. On the other hand, the individuals themselves are entirely subordinated to the division of labour and hence are brought into the most complete dependence on one another. Private property, insofar as within labour itself it is opposed to labour, evolves out of the necessity of accumulation, and has still, to begin with, rather the form of the communality; but in its further development it approaches more and more the modern form of private property. The division of labour implies from the outset the division of the *conditions* of labour, of tools and materials, and thus the splitting-up of accumulated capital among different owners, and thus, also, the division between capital and labour, and the different forms of property itself. The more the division of labour develops and accumulation grows, the sharper are the forms that this process of differentiation assumes. Labour itself can only exist on the premise of this fragmentation.

Thus two facts are here revealed. First the productive forces appear as a world for themselves, quite independent of and divorced from the individuals, alongside the individuals: the reason for this is that the individuals, whose forces they are, are split up and in opposition to one another, whilst, on the other hand, these forces are only real forces in the intercourse and association of these individuals. Thus, on the one hand, we have a totality of productive forces, which have, as it were, taken on a material form and are for the individuals no longer the forces of the individuals but of private property, and hence of the individuals only insofar as they are owners of private property themselves. Never, in any earlier period, have the productive forces taken on a form so indifferent to the intercourse of individuals *as* individuals, because their intercourse itself was formerly a restricted one. On the other hand, standing over against these productive forces, we have the majority of the individuals, from whom these forces have been wrested away, and who, robbed thus of all real life-content, have become abstract individuals, but who are, however, only by this fact put into a position to enter into relation with one another *as individuals*.

The only connection which still links them with the productive forces and with their own existence – labour – has lost all semblance of self-activity and only sustain their life by stunting it. While in the earlier periods self-activity and the production of material life were separated, in that they devolved on different persons, and while, on account of the narrowness of the individuals themselves, the production of material life was considered as a subordinate mode of self-activity, they now diverge to such an extent that altogether material life appears as the end, and what produces this material life, labour (which is now the only possible but, as we see, negative form of self-activity), as the means.

Thus things have now come to such a pass that the individuals must appropriate the existing totality of productive forces, not only to achieve self-activity, but, also, merely to safeguard their very existence. This appropriation is first determined by the object to be appropriated, the productive forces, which have been developed to a totality and which only exist within a universal intercourse. From this aspect alone, therefore, this appropriation must have a universal character corresponding to the productive forces and the intercourse.

The appropriation of these forces is itself nothing more than the development of the individual capacities corresponding to the material instruments of production. The appropriation of a totality of instruments of production is, for this very reason, the development of a totality of capacities in the individuals themselves.

This appropriation is further determined by the persons appropriating. Only the proletarians of the present day, who are completely shut off from all self-activity, are in a position to achieve a complete and no longer restricted self-activity, which consists in the appropriation of a totality of productive forces and in the thus postulated development of a totality of capacities. All earlier revolutionary appropriations were restricted; individuals, whose self-activity was restricted by a crude instrument of production and a limited intercourse, appropriated this crude instrument of production, and hence merely achieved a new state of limitation. Their instrument of production became their property, but they themselves remained subordinate to the division of labour and their own instrument of production. In all expropriations up to now, a mass of individuals remained subservient to a single instrument of production; in the appropriation by the proletarians, a mass of instruments of production must be made subject to each individual, and property to all. Modern universal intercourse can be controlled by individuals, therefore, only when controlled by all.

This appropriation is further determined by the manner in which it must be effected. It can only be effected through a union, which by the character of the proletariat itself can again only be a universal one, and through a revolution, in which, on the one hand, the power of the earlier mode of production and intercourse and social organisation is overthrown, and, on the other hand, there develops the universal character and the energy of the proletariat, without which the revolution cannot be accomplished; and in which, further, the proletariat rids itself of everything that still clings to it from its previous position in society.

Only at this stage does self-activity coincide with material life, which corresponds to the developments of individuals into complete individuals and the casting-off of all natural limitations. The transformation of labour into self-activity corresponds to the transformation of the earlier limited intercourse into the intercourse of individuals as such. With the appropriation of the total productive forces through united individuals, private property comes to an end. Whilst previously in history a particular condition always appeared as accidental, now the isolation of individuals and the particular private gain of each man have themselves become accidental.

The individuals, who are no longer subject to the division of labour, have been conceived by the philosophers as an ideal, under the name 'Man'. They have conceived the whole process which we have outlined as the evolutionary process of 'Man', so that at every historical stage 'Man' was substituted for the individuals and shown as the motive force of history. The whole process was thus conceived as a process of the self-estrangement of 'Man', and this was essentially due to the fact that the average individual of the later stage was always foisted on to the earlier stage, and the consciousness of a later age on to the individuals of an earlier. Through this inversion, which from the first is an abstract image of the actual conditions, it was possible to transform the whole of history into an evolutionary process of consciousness.

Finally, from the conception of history we have sketched we obtain these further conclusions: (1) In the development of productive forces there comes a stage when productive forces and means of intercourse are brought into being, which, under the existing relationships, only cause mischief, and are no longer productive but destructive forces (machinery and money); and connected with this a class is called forth, which has to bear all the burdens of society without enjoying its advantages, which, ousted from society, is forced into the most decided antagonism to all other classes; a class which form the majority of all members of society, and from which emanates the consciousness of the necessity of a fundamental revolution, the communist consciousness, which may, of course, arise among the other classes too through the contemplation of the situation of this class. (2) The conditions under which definite productive forces can be applied are the conditions of the rule of a definite class of society, whose social power, deriving from its property, has its *practical*-idealistic expression in each case in the form of the State; and, therefore, every revolutionary struggle is directed against a class, which till then has been in power.[1] (3) In all revolutions up till now the mode of activity always remained unscathed and it was only a question of a different distribution of this activity, a new distribution of labour to other persons, whilst the communist revolution is directed against the preceding *mode* of activity, does away with *labour*, and abolishes the rule of all classes with the classes themselves, because it is carried through by the class which no longer counts as a class in society, is not recognised as a class, and is in itself the expression of the dissolution of all classes, nationalities, etc. within present society; and (4) Both for the production on a mass scale of this communist consciousness, and for the success of the cause itself, the alteration of men on a mass scale is, necessary, an alteration which can only take place in a practical movement, a *revolution*; this revolution is necessary, therefore, not only because the *ruling* class cannot be overthrown in any other way, but also because the class *overthrowing* it can only in a revolution succeed in ridding itself of all the muck of ages and become fitted to found society anew.

NOTE

1. [*Marginal note by Marx:*] The people are interested in maintaining the present state of production.

FURTHER READING

For people who want to understand more of Marx and Engels' general theory, the best starting points are:

A. Callinicos, *The Revolutionary Ideas of Karl Marx*, London: Bookmarks, 1996.

K. Marx and F. Engels, *The German Ideology*, C.J. Arthur (ed), London: Lawrence and Wishart, 1999

K. Marx, *The Communist Manifesto*, London: Lawrence and Wishart, 1990.

Marx's Capital, A Student Edition, C.J. Arthur (ed), London: Lawrence & Wishart, 1992

K. Marx, Selected Works in One Volume, London: Lawrence and Wishart, 1991

F. Wheen, *Karl Marx*, London: Fourth Estate, 1999.

Lawrence and Wishart publish the 50-volume collected works.

In addition to the sources mentioned in the footnotes I would also recommend:

N. Chomsky, *Rogue States*, London: Pluto, 2000.

K. Danaher and R. Burbach (ed), *Globalize This!*, New York: Common Courage Press, 2000.

K. Danaher (ed), *Democratizing the Global Economy*, New York: Common Courage Press, 2001.

J.B. Foster, *Marx's Ecology*, New York: Monthly Review Press, 2000.

S. George, *The Lugano Report*, London: Pluto, 1999.

J. Gray, *False Dawn: The Delusions of Global Capitalism*, London: Granta, 1998.

P. Hirst and G. Thompson, *Globalisation in Question*, Cambridge: Polity, 1996.

R. Kiely and P. Marfleet, *Globalisation and the Third World*, London: Routledge, 1998.

N. Klein, *No Logo*, London: Flamingo, 2000.

K. Moody, *Workers in a Lean World*, London and New York: Verso, 1997.